To MaryKate
May you capture the joy
of living and learning as
seen through Molly May's eyes!
Rewa
5-10-08

Molly May
on the
T̶C Ranch

Molly May on the **TC** Ranch

by
Rewa

Illustration by Karry Brown
Photo usage by permission

Little Red Cat Publishing 2002

Published by Little Red Cat Publishing

LIBRARY OF CONGRESS CATALOGING-IN-PUBLICATION DATA

Rewa
     Molly May on the TC Ranch
       p. cm.

Summary: Book 2 in a series. The continuing story of a young girl, Molly May, and her adventures on a ranch in South Dakota in the early 1920's.

     ISBN X-XXXXX-XXX-X

1. Ranch Life   2. Ranch Life - Black Hills Region, South Dakota 3. Children 4. South Dakota - Social Life and Customs
5. Autobiography I. Rewa II. Title

Autobio.   02-XXXXXX

THE AUTHOR

I am Molly May. When I was twenty-one I started to write for publication and I used another of my real names "Rewa" under which I do most of my writing.

3 years old, in Ceylon

DEDICATION

To Edward, Christy & Robinette
I have been truly blessed!
Love you, Mom

ACKNOWLEDGEMENTS

I am grateful to my granddaughter, Lisa Westmoreland, for her encouragement and many writing suggestions.

To Shirley Haggin and Elsa Heald who so generously made time to proof read.

To members of the Satellite Critique Group.

To Esther Davis, Margaret Hengle, and Caryn Yacowitz for their kind back-cover endorsements.

Molly May
on the TC Ranch

My body may be nourished by a nutritious diet, but my soul feasts on the smorgasbord of my memories.

CONTENTS

PREFACE

For fourteen days six-year-old Molly May had travelled alone on the Olympic, sistership to the Titanic. Then she rode on American trains jiggety-jogging past forests of snow-covered trees and immense, flat, lonely, empty fields. Occasionally the train would come to a grinding halt at a train station to unload people

 and baggage. Soon similar scenery would appear again. Would she ever arrive at Aunt Georgie's and Uncle Ed's?

On November 5, 1922 she finally arrived at their Cattle Ranch in the Black Hills of South Dakota. Upon first glance she liked Aunt Georgie and Uncle Ed, but her days in an English orphanage had taught her not to trust people, she could always be sent back.

* * *

"Molly May, I'm sure you are tired from your long journey," Aunt Georgie said after many hugs of welcome. "We'll put your baggage in our bedroom. Tonight you will sleep on a cot at the foot of our bed. You may hang your coat on a hook over there," Aunt Georgie pointed to a coat-rack close to the parlor door. "I have your coat tag you won't need it anymore."

Molly May shyly glanced around, finding everything very strange. The room was large, but she noticed a piano in a corner. That meant there would be singing, which Molly May loved. Something was making a crackling sound from a big round stove; she would be warm this cloudy, rainy day. Across the room from the stove were two large chairs with pillow-like seats and backs. She imagined herself curled up in one of them to read some of the shelf-of-books nearby. Would this, at last, be her new home?

"Uncle Ed and I hope this will be your home for a long time. Would you like that?"

"Yes," Molly May whispered in a tiny voice as she continued to look around the large room.

"How long do you think you'd like to stay?" Aunt Georgie asked.

Molly May's voice and courage came back. "I'll stay a fortnight if that's all right. I think the orphanage may expect me back by then."

"Well, we'll see how you like the ranch." Aunt Georgie gave a questioning glance at Uncle Ed.

"I'll get Molly May's bag from the buggy," Uncle Ed remarked. "I'm ready for tea and that special carrot cake you made for Molly May's welcome."

SPLISH, SPLASH, SPLOSH

After enjoying tea and the special welcome carrot cake that smelled and tasted so good, Aunt Georgie remarked, "You had a very long voyage and train journey. I'm sure you would like a bath.

"Uncle Ed will set up the bathtub in our parlor in front of our potbelly wood burning stove. It keeps our whole house warm and will keep you warm for your bath. I'll wash your hair in the washstand in my bedroom."

Molly May frowned. "I don't want my hair washed. One of the older girls at the orphanage always washed my hair. When she did, she always pulled it and I got soap in my eyes. I'll let you do it another day."

Molly May's stay in the orphanage had taught her to obey adults, but sometimes she was an impudent little girl. She had been spoiled on the Olympic ship by the adults giving her a lot of attention. She needed to remember her Aunty Belle's instruction: 'Little girls should be seen, not heard'.

"I'm sorry, Molly May, but I noticed some lice in your hair. I must wash your hair immediately."

Aunt Georgie was lucky to have some Tea Tree Oil to use to get rid of the lice. She had some friends who came from Turkey. The

15

Immigration Doctor noticed their two little girls had lice so they had to have their heads shaved. She didn't want to do that to Molly May. She knew she had to wash Molly May's hair immediately with the Tea Tree Oil to get rid of the lice. It was fortunate that Molly May's lice had not been noticed at Immigration.

"Mrs. Cole told me the doctor said I was healthy." Molly May pouted. "I don't need my hair washed."

"I'll be very careful, Molly May. Your hair looks like a bird's nest, but I won't pull your hair and I'll be careful of your eyes, too."

Molly May sulked. "Are lice what's making my head itch?"

"Yes! Lice are little insects that get into people's hair when their hair is not washed often. The lice make a person's head itch. They don't have wings so they can't fly away. They are very difficult to get rid of and sometimes take many washings. We MUST wash your hair immediately to get rid of the little rascals."

"All right Aunt Georgie," Molly May pushed out her lips. "Promise to be careful, though."

"I promise! Your hair is straight, shall we make curls for tomorrow?"

"CURLS? Can you really give me curls?" Molly May's anxiety melted away. "I don't like my straight brown hair. Can you really make my hair curly?"

"I heard that conversation," Uncle Ed said as he carried in a big, round, shiny metal tub and set it down in front of the large pot-belly iron stove. "I can tell you how to get curls, Molly May. It's by magic! That's right, magic, wait and see."

"Now Ed," Aunt Georgie laughed. "Off with you before you have Molly May in a dither. Please put two kettles of water on the kitchen stove to heat.

"For curls, Molly May, your hair must be clean."

Molly May's lips turned to a smile. "On the big ship, Olympic, my friend Sarah was so pretty. She had long golden curls. I twisted my hair around my fingers, but it wouldn't make curls. Tell me," Molly May begged. "How do I get curls?"

"The curls are called 'Rag Curls'. I'll tie up small bunches of your hair in short rags. You'll have to sleep with them on your head. In the morning, when you awake I'll untie the rags. Your hair will be curly. It is magic, all right, magic!"

"Promise not to pull, promise, Aunt Georgie. Will I look funny?"

"No, you won't look funny. Only Uncle Ed and I will see you, and we know you won't look funny.

"Ed, please fill the bathtub," Aunt Georgie called. "The head-wash won't take long.

"Use this washcloth to cover your eyes, Molly May. I won't get soap in them." Shampoo bubbles and suds felt fresh, soft and clean in Aunt Georgie's hands as she gently scrubbed Molly May's head. "That felt good, Aunt Georgie, please do some more."

"Now the rinse. I hope the Tea Tree Oil will make the lice go away. Here is a towel. Your bath is ready. Here's your soap and wash cloth, and remember to rinse well. To dry I'll warm this big towel for you in the kitchen stove oven."

On the ranch baths were not every night, only in summer. In the winter it was usual to bathe twice a week, unless one got very dirty. Aunt Georgie hugged the towel-wrapped Molly May. Molly May got into her nightie, ready for magic curls to be made.

"Your curls will only last a day or two. If you like them and don't mind sleeping in the rags, we can put your hair in them every bath night."

Aunt Georgie gathered a pile of torn sheet rags about four inches long. She brushed Molly May's hair, took a comb and parted a small hair-strand, then tied the rag around it.

"Ow! that rag is tight. The rags seem to pull my hair, but I don't mind. I want curls!"

Uncle Ed stood by the kitchen door watching the parlor activity. "What is that 'Ow' all about?" he asked. "If you want to have magic curls you will have to expect a few 'Ows'!"

"I'm finished," Aunt Georgie said. "Tomorrow is CURLS DAY!"

With hugs and kisses Aunt Georgie and Uncle Ed said, "Good night. Sweet dreams! Tomorrow the magic curls will be yours."

CURLS

The next morning Molly May's cot was smothered in sunshine coming from the big bedroom window. She stretched, then sat up with a start. What was on her head? Her hands went past her shoulders, past her cheeks, up to her head. "My rag curls, that's what! The curls that Aunt Georgie made last night! Do I have curls? Aunt Georgie! Aunt Georgie! Do I have curls? Do I have curls?"

"Oh good! You're awake. Wrap this blanket around you and come into the kitchen where it's warm. I'll give you a looking glass to watch me unwrap the curls." Molly May found a chair by the stove while Aunt Georgie unwrapped the rags for her Magic curls.

Curls meant a lot to Molly May. Her first day on the Olympic ship she had seen another little girl like herself on the deck before the Olympic ship sailed. That little girl had long golden curls.

She tried to get over to her, but the forest of legs from grown-ups prevented her. Molly May didn't find the little girl with the golden curls until three days later when they met on the Promenade Deck. Her name was Sarah.

Now, with Aunt Georgie's knowledge and nimble fingers, Molly May had curls, real Curls!

One by one Molly May's straight brown hair strands had become Molly May's curly brown hair. She squealed with happiness as she put all ten fingers to her hair pulling the curls in and out and back to her head. "Oh Aunt Georgie! How wonderful!

They really are Magic curls!"

Molly May's curls would not last forever. Rag curls have to be worn about every second or third night. But soon, with Aunt Georgie's magic, the lice in Molly May's head would disappear and Rag Curls would become an evening event at bath time, every two or three evenings.

"I'm glad you're happy, Molly May. Please get dressed so we can have breakfast. Your baggage is by your cot. I noticed you have another set of clothes, though I have bought you a dress or two that you can fit on later."

As she dressed she played with her curls and looked out of the large bedroom window by her cot. There was a blanket of snow wherever she looked. Nature had even made the pine trees beautiful with thick patches of snow on the branches. While she was looking a crow flew on a branch. His landing shook the snow off that branch. It made Molly May giggle.

The day was still sunny with a bright blue sky. The world stood still. Everything seemed soft and gentle. Her eyes became misty. Was she dreaming? Her shaking hands reached to her head again. Yes! Curls! What would Sarah, her Olympic friend, say if she saw Molly May with curls? Would she live in this house a long time? How long would Aunt Georgie and Uncle Ed keep her? She had come so far, would she be sent back to the orphanage?

"Breakfast is ready, Molly May," Aunt Georgie called from the kitchen. "Your chair is here by a kitchen window where you can see things that look like weeds poking up through the snow."

BREAKFAST

"Thank you, I'm hungry." Molly May answered, as she took the seat by the window that Aunt Georgie had pointed to. "I hope it's not gruel and treacle. None of us in the orphanage liked it, but we had it all the time, and we had to eat it. The Olympic ship had lots and lots of different foods to try. I had a difficult time choosing."

"No, Molly May, no gruel and treacle. Uncle Ed doesn't like it either. Today we have porridge with raisins, his favorite. Some mornings I put in dates; they both make the porridge sweet. I hope you like raisins. We will also have some of my homemade wheat bread toasted and served with real English orange marmalade made from oranges that come from Portugal. And, of course, we always have a nice big glass of milk from last night's milking."

"I remember once we had raisins for a treat. One of the girls asked Sister Frances what animal gave us raisins and everybody laughed. I didn't think that was nice to make fun of her, it made her cry."

As Molly May watched, Aunt Georgie scurried around in the kitchen. "Here is your porridge with raisins, and a nice slice of toasted bread. Try the marmalade on it, I think you'll like it."

Molly May sampled the porridge, and smacked her lips. "The porridge is delicious, Aunt Georgie, and I like the raisins in it. Do you have a raisin tree and a date tree?"

"No, raisins are dried from grapes that are harvested from the

grapes left on the vines after most of the grapes are picked for wine making. Dates are the fruit of a palm tree. We don't have either grape vines or a palm tree."

Aunt Georgie wore a pretty light blue apron that covered the front of her dress and tied in the back. It had two large darker blue pockets. On them were embroidered yellow, orange and red flowers.

She was cooking on a big iron stove. She kept putting wood into one side and water was steaming out of the other side. The middle of the stove seemed to be the main cooking area. Here she stirred the pot of porridge, and a kettle was steaming.

"I like your homemade bread and marmalade, too. I had an orange once, it was very good."

"You may have all you want, and here is a bowl of sliced bananas. We always like to have some fruit for breakfast. We don't want you to be hungry."

24

Molly May finished her breakfast and looked out of the window. There she saw some small red and green round things, some yellowy-orange big round things, and some green stalk-like tall and skinny things poking through the snow on the ground. What she liked best were the pretty yellow, red and orange flowers that were shaped like small bells.

"What are all these other things, Aunt Georgie? They don't look like weeds."

"Oh! I forgot, you are right, they are not weeds, they are the remains of my vegetable garden. The red and green small round things are tomatoes that I will use to make green tomato jam, the orange are pumpkins to make pies, and the green stalk-like things are green onions. The only thing really growing now are my Nasturtium flowers. Aren't they pretty? I embroidered them on my apron pockets." She held out her apron for Molly May to see. "You may cut a bouquet if you like."

Aunt Georgie opened a drawer in a kitchen counter and placed a pair of scissors beside Molly May's plate.

"After you finish your breakfast here are the scissors. Please be careful cutting the flowers, the scissors are very sharp. Cut the flowers with a stem to fit this vase," she said as she put a vase down beside her.

"I'll clean up the kitchen. When we're both through we'll go upstairs to inspect your room."

"My room, Aunt Georgie? Do you have a dormitory?"

"My goodness no, Molly May, our house doesn't have a

POPEYE

Suddenly there were noisy sounds. The kitchen door opened loudly and Uncle Ed unloaded his arms of firewood. Logs tumbled in every direction, but Aunt Georgie didn't seem to mind, she just kept on stirring a pot of porridge. Then a large shaggy ball of fur raced up to the kitchen door.

"What is that?" Molly May gasped.

"I'll let you come in and meet Molly May if you behave," Uncle

Ed told the large shaggy ball of fur.

"Molly May, let me introduce Popeye. He is part retriever and part sheep dog. Sit, Popeye," Uncle Ed commanded as he opened the door.

Molly May drew back in her chair. "He's big," she stammered.

"He won't hurt you," Uncle Ed assured her. "Give Molly May your paw-shake, Popeye." The dog held up his paw.

Molly May gingerly took his lifted paw and shook it. Popeye shuffled his body closer to her, flopping his shaggy head onto her lap, as Molly May broke into gales of laughter.

Popeye was known by the local ranchers as a friendly dog and

27

very good with the cattle by helping herd them into the corral from the pastures and range. He barked at their heels, but they didn't seem to mind.

"That is a funny name for a dog, Uncle Ed. I can't see his eyes," Molly May commented.

"Well, he has eyes. I don't know how he can see with all that fur hanging over them. They are pop eyes all right."

Popeye lifted his head and thumped his tail on the kitchen floor: thump! thump!

If I didn't know better I'd think he was a talking dog, Uncle Ed." Again Molly May broke into gales of laughter as she petted him. "Ouch! That prickled!"

"That was from a cocklebur in his fur. Some people call them 'stickyburs'. Popeye gets them in his fur when he runs after the cattle on our range. It takes time to get them out.

"Don't worry, Molly May. He will be your best friend before you know it. He will take good care of you."

"If I have to go back to the orphanage may I take Popeye with me? I like him very much."

"We're not planning to send you back," Uncle Ed said, giving Molly May a big hug. "Also, I'm afraid Popeye is too old for that long journey."

"We're ready now, Molly May. We've finished in the kitchen," Aunt Georgie said. "I want to show you your room."

A ROOM OF HER OWN

Molly May could not believe what she saw. This room was going to be her very own? Her eyes opened wide, her jaw dropped.

"A room of my very own, Aunt Georgie?" She pirouetted in excitement, then suddenly slowed down trying to place everything. At the orphanage she had only her bed and one dresser drawer for her clothes. There were eight of them in the dormitory. It wasn't this big, here there was so much to see.

This room had one light blue wall with small bunches of different colored flowers all over, like flower pictures. The other walls were painted white that made the room look large and clean.

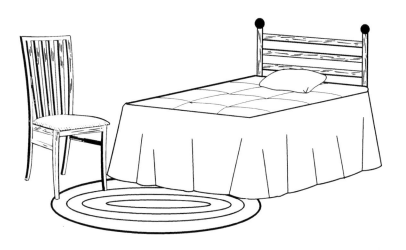

"Yes, Molly May, you will have a room of your very own. I chose blue for your blanket and eiderdown quilt. Try lying down."

As Molly May lay down she sunk deep and almost disappeared in the thick, soft eiderdown quilt.

"Can you find me in here, Aunt Georgie?" Molly May giggled. "It is a good hiding place."

"Yes, I see you, but you are not very big so I think the eiderdown quilt will cover you and keep you nice and warm.

"I put up blue curtains to match your quilt. Come and look out of the window."

Molly May hugged Aunt Georgie. "Blue is my favorite color. And a window! There was a window in the orphanage dormitory, but it was very high, near the ceiling. I couldn't see out of it even standing on my tippy-toes."

This window looked out on a fenced area with the remains of lettuce, peas, green beans, squash and tomato plants that had been a summer garden. A few marigolds and yellow and orange nasturtiums still bloomed, a sign of winter soon arriving.

"Do you like vegetables, Molly May?"

"I'm not sure. I only remember having gruel and treacle, once in awhile an egg."

"We like vegatables. When you try them I think that you'll like them, too. Right now let's look at your furniture." Aunt Georgie put her hand on a brown piece of furniture with three drawers on one side. She pulled out another drawer in the desk center which held some pencils.

"Sister Frances wrote me you could read and write very well. She told me you also know all your arithmetic times-tables. Is that true?"

"Yes, I like arithmetic. Times-tables are fun." Molly May rattled off tens. "Tens are easiest. Reading and writing stories is my favorite schoolwork."

"I'm glad you like to read. I have many books. This door opens your closet, and the chest of drawers, for your clothes, is on the other side. Open the door. There's a surprise for you."

Molly May excitedly but slowly peaked in as she opened the closet door. There before her were two hangers with the most beautiful dresses Molly May had ever seen.

One was a pink rose color with tiny rose embroidery scattered here and there. The other was pale blue with darker ocean-blue ribbon trim.

She gasped. "Where did these come from, Aunt Georgie?" She gently ran her hand over the soft material fingering each dress with its matching petticoat and panties.

"One of your cousins, Beatrice, made them for you. She wanted to surprise you. These are to be worn for very special occasions."

"They're the most beautiful dresses I've ever seen." Molly May shook her head with disbelief. "What will I look like in different clothes every day? That's hard to think about, Aunt Georgie."

"You'll look very nice. You have worn a uniform long enough. We will put it away forever. I have bought some clothes for you, also. We will try these on and the new ones I have purchased for you a little later. I need to go downstairs to the kitchen now. You may stay here and get acquainted with your room if you like."

Molly May sat down at the desk. She found a pencil and some paper in a drawer. She started to try to draw her bed, then a window with plants outside. Not satisfied she wrinkled the paper into a ball and started again, but scratched it up. "I can't draw this wonderful room of my very own with the special dresses," she said out loud. "I'm going to surprise Aunt Georgie with not a picture but a Thank you letter. I love Aunt Georgie."

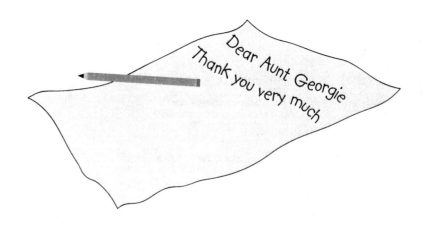

MOLLY MAY'S BIRTHDAY

"I know you are six-and-three-quarters-almost seven, Molly May, but I don't know your birthdate," Aunt Georgie remarked one morning. "When is your birthday?"

"My 'Happy Birthday' and 'Happy New Year' is the thirteenth, fourteenth and fifteenth of March. When are yours and Uncle Ed's special days?" Molly May put her hand over her mouth to stop talking. She remembered Aunty Belle always said 'you should be seen, not heard'.

"Mine is in May and Uncle Ed's is in February," Aunt Georgie replied. "You know you can't have three birthdays, Molly May. We only celebrate one birthday in a year. And what do you mean by 'Happy New Year'? That is January first of each year."

"All I know, Aunt Georgie, is that when Sister Frances came to the orphanage she started the five Birthday/New Year rules for the orphanage children. We learned that our birthday was the start of our very own New Year. She told us it was the most important day of our lives. The New Year gave us a new start so we could become better children. If Sister Frances decided we had met all the rules, then we deserved to celebrate. Everyone would say 'Happy New Year' to us as well as 'Happy Birthday'."

"I've recited the rules two times so far because I started at four years old and now I'm six," Molly May said.

"A few days before birthday time we had to recite the five rules to Sister Frances. If she passed us, we could keep our birthday. It

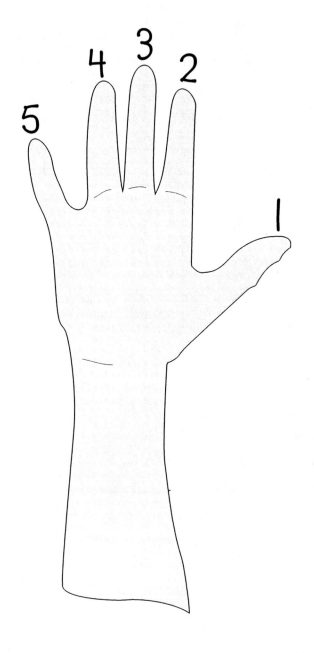

was always three days." Molly May spoke and counted the Five Birthday/New Year Rules off on her fingers.

"Number 1: I have been polite and remembered my manners.

Number 2: I have kept myself neat and clean.

Number 3: I have had good school grades.

Number 4: I have been obedient.

Number 5: I have done my orphanage cleaning chores properly.

"All of us wondered what would happen if Sister Frances said 'No'." Molly May's voice quivered. "No one dared misbehave."

"Sometimes it is necessary to know the exact day you were born," Aunt Georgie explained. "I will write Sister Frances and see if she has a record of your true birth date."

Molly May's voice became a whisper, she didn't want to lose her three birthdays and New Year. "Does that mean I'll only have one birthday and no New Year in America?"

"No! No!" Aunt Georgie hugged her. 'Your 'Happy Birthday' and 'Happy New Year' will always be your three days in March with us. I think maybe Uncle Ed and I would like to celebrate three days for ours, too. Shall we do that?"

"Oh yes, Aunt Georgie." Molly May sighed with relief. "But who will you ask if you can 'keep your birthday'?"

"I hadn't thought about that. We'll find out if Uncle Ed can come up with a solution!"

COUSIN JEAN

Burrring, buring, buring. Burrrring, buring, buring. "That's our telephone bell, one long and two short," Aunt Georgie said when she heard the sound.

"Hello, hello, are you there? Hello. That's wonderful. Come early. I'll have our noon hour dinner ready. We'll be waiting."

"I have exciting news, Molly May," Aunt Georgie said, hanging up the telephone. "That was Irene calling. She and Philip would like to come to the $\bar{C}$ Ranch tomorrow with Jean. They are your cousins and especially want to meet you.

"Jean is four years old. You and she will have fun playing together. I think she is very pretty.

"You will like Irene. She is pretty also, but with dark brown hair and eyes.

"Philip you will find a lot of fun. He likes to play jokes on people and he plays games with Jean. His friends call him a cowboy because he rides wild horses in Country Fairs and Rodeos."

Buring, buring, buring rang the telephone again. "That telephone bell, three short rings, is for the Bale Ranch," Aunt Georgie explained. "I can pick the receiver off the hook and listen, but that wouldn't be nice or polite, Molly May. We won't worry about the telephone. We must get ready for your cousins."

They lived about fifteen miles from the $\bar{C}$ Ranch on their own ranch called Southfork. They would come in their big buggy so Philip and Irene could go to Buffalo Gap tomorrow for supplies.

Jean would stay with Molly May so they could play and get acquainted.

Molly May tried not to sound excited, but her insides jumped up and down as she clapped her hands. "Do they know Popeye, the dog, and all the other ranch animals?" She could hardly wait to show Jean her doll, Lizbeth.

"May I show Jean my room, Aunt Georgie?"

"Of course. We'll put a cot in your room so she can sleep with you. Everyone will be staying overnight."

Molly May's insides started to curl from excitement. "I'll love having Jean sleep in my room. We'll try to be very quiet. I learned to be quiet in the orphanage. We were given a bad mark if we were noisy and caught talking or laughing after 'lights out'."

Indian Hill could be seen from the parlor windows. Tomorrow Molly May could watch for their big buggy to start down the hill. When the sun shone Indian Hill looked beautiful with its many evergreen trees sparkling in a splash of sunshine.

***

The next morning everyone was up early. Molly May watched at the window for their big buggy to start down Indian Hill. Soon she spotted it. It didn't take very long before it clattered into the front yard which was covered with snow.

"They're here! They're here! Aunt Georgie, they're here!" Molly May ran to the kitchen, grabbed Aunt Georgie's hand and

38

pulled her to the parlor door.

Aunt Georgie gave everyone a big hug and kiss. Uncle Ed lifted Jean, squealing and giggling with excitement, high above his head.

Molly May suddenly stepped behind the kitchen door. With squinty eyes she peaked out cautiously.

"Molly May! Molly May!" Aunt Georgie called. "My goodness, she was just here. Molly May! Molly May! Where are you?" Molly May slowly and shyly came into the parlor. Aunt Georgie hugged her.

"Philip, Irene, and Jean, meet Molly May, your cousin from England. She has come to live with PaPa and me. She has been having a lot of fun discovering the ⟨ Ranch."

"How-do-you-do," Molly May curtsied, as she had been taught to do at the orphanage whenever she met an adult.

Jean mimicked her.

"We don't need formality here," Aunt Georgie laughed. "Relatives know each other at first glance."

Suddenly Molly May squeezed Aunt Georgie's hand to keep from shaking. Embarrassingly she clutched Aunt Georgie's apron and peeked out from it, almost covering her face.

Aunt Georgie took her shaking hand. "Jean is part of your family, Molly May. You don't need to be shy. Don't you want to show Jean your doll Lizbeth and your room? Dinner isn't ready yet. I'll call you."

Molly May glanced at Jean and whispered. "I have a room of my very own. Would you like to see it?"

Jean held out her hand to Molly May. They took hands and climbed the stairs to Molly May's room.

NEW CLOTHES

"Here is my room," Molly May shyly told Jean as they got to the top of the stairs. "Do you have a room of your own?" Molly May asked as she opened the door.

"Yes, but it won't be for very long because Mommy is going to have a baby for me to play with. The baby will live with me in my room. Mommy has been fixing a special place for the baby's bed."

"Where is she going to get the baby? I'd like that. Maybe Aunt Georgie can find one for me?"

"That would be nice, then we'd have two babies to play with."

"Here is Lizbeth, my doll." Molly May walked over to a chair and carefully handed Lizbeth to Jean's out-stretched arms.

"Hold her tight, her dress is silky-soft, shiny, and slippery." The words untangled from her tongue.

"I brought my doll with me. I'll show her to you when we go downstairs. I call her Mary. She isn't as pretty as Lizbeth. Mary's body is soft, but her face looks a little bit like our face."

"That's nice, then we can play dolls together. Do you have a closet for your clothes in your room?"

"Yes, but it is full of things for the baby."

"Would you like to see my new dresses? Cousin Bea made them for me. Here they are. Which one would you like to try on first?"

Jean's eyes opened wide as she looked at the two different colored dresses hanging in front of her. Each had a petticoat and panties to match.

"It 's hard to choose, but I like pink. It looks too big for me. You put it on, Molly May."

"I haven't had time to fit either of them on yet. I think they are for special times like a party. Aunt Georgie bought this dress that I'm wearing. She said it is called an 'Apron Dress'. I don't know what that means, but I like the pockets. Feel this decoration on the collar, Jean."

Molly May took Jean's hand and placed it on the embroidery. The embroidery looked like pockets, but you couldn't put your hand in it. It was part of the dress.

Jean giggled. "Do you have anything in your pockets? I have something in mine, but it's a secret. I'll tell you, if you will guess."

Molly May reached into one of her pockets. Her hand came out slowly, but it was closed tight. "Guess which hand has something in it, Jean. If you guess it right, you can have it."

"All right, it's that hand," Jean said as she pointed to the left. "It's a piece of candy."

"That's a good guess. Here is your candy. Now you tell me what is in your pocket."

Jean copied Molly May and slowly reached into one of her dress pockets, but kept her hand closed. "It's your turn to guess now".

"It's a penny?"

"No."

"It's a piece of candy?"

"No."

"I give up."

"It's a button off your dress. I found it on the floor."

Molly May's hand flew up to her collar. One side of her dress had a button on the embroidery, but the other side had a button missing. It was a good thing it was found as Aunt Georgie might have been cross if it was lost.

"Let me show you some more clothes she bought me." Molly May opened a dresser drawer. "She said this is called a 'Khaki Play Outfit', and I have to grow into it. I don't know what she means. I'm glad it is too big for me right now, because I don't think it is very pretty."

The dress had two pieces, the top was a shirt, the bottom piece was pants, but they were called Knickers, and had pockets.

"My favorite, except for Cousin Bea's dresses, is this dress." Molly May opened another drawer and shook out a navy-blue dress with white trim and a red bow.

"This is called a 'Sailor Dress'. I saw sailors with collars like this on their shirts when I was on the Olympic ship. I like the skirt part best because Aunt Georgie said it has pleats so I could skip and hop around. Aunt Georgie said it was like dancing.

"Sarah, my friend on the Olympic ship, showed me how to dance. Her dresses were very beautiful, like the ones Cousin Bea made me. We had a party on the ship."

All of a sudden Molly May got very quiet. With a sad voice she said, "When I think or talk about the Olympic ship I get afraid." Her voice shook. "I'm going to be very, very good so I can stay with Aunt Georgie and Uncle Ed. Then they won't send me back to the orphanage. I love them a lot. I want to be here forever. I love you too, Jean." Molly May hugged her.

"MaMa won't send you away." Jean said about Aunt Georgie. "She is my Grandmother. I call her 'MaMa', and I love her, she won't send you away."

"Aunt Georgie says you are my cousin," Molly May told Jean. "We belong to the same family. Let's pretend we're going to a party. We can take our dolls, too. But we'll all have to dress up. You can wear one of my Cousin Bea's dresses. We can make it fit you."

"That sounds like fun, Molly May."

* * *

"Molly May and Jean, dinner is ready," Aunt Georgie called. "You may play another visit time."

FEEDING FEATHERED FRIENDS

Molly May sat bolt upright in her bed. All of a sudden she had an exciting idea! She bounced out of bed, opened the curtains to let in the sunshine, and dressed as quickly as she could.

Would Aunt Georgie let her feed the chickens, ducks, turkeys, and geese today? She knew she could do it! They wouldn't peck her. She was too big! But she knew she'd have to be careful of the geese. They were big birds.

"Aunt Georgie, Aunt Georgie!" she called as she flew down the stairs. "May I feed the chickens, ducks, turkeys, and geese today? I'm not afraid. They won't peck me. I'm too big."

Aunt Georgie looked surprised. "Well, I don't know why not. Everyone here on the Ⅎ Ranch does something special. If you would like to do that as your special duty, then so be it. Uncle Ed or I will go with you for the first time or two."

"I'd like that." Molly May skipped around the room. "It will be fun, Aunt Georgie. May we start this morning?"

"Uncle Ed feeds all the animals, particularly our feathered friends, very early in the morning. They are always hungry so we will give them some more food. It's quite cold. We'll need our coats, caps and scarfs."

Aunt Georgie walked to the coat rack in the hall to get her winter clothes, but first she put on a large blue apron that she wore when feeding the feathered friends. On the apron in the front and on large pockets were different embroidered barnyard birds in their natural colors. Across the front at the top were the words 'Feeding Feathered Friends'.

Molly May was mesmerized. "Aunt Georgie that is the most beautiful apron I have ever seen."

"I'm glad you like it, Molly May. It's my favorite. Your cousin, Bea, who likes to embroider, made it for me."

"May we use the stile instead of the gate?" Molly May asked as they walked toward the barnyard.

When Molly May was in the orphanage Sister Frances took the children into her flower garden on holidays. She told them that the garden was a special and beautiful place. They used the stile instead of the gate because the children liked going up the three steps and down the three steps over the fence into the garden.

"The stile makes me think I'm entering a special place," Molly May said.

"You're right, the barnyard is a special place."

"Also, when I was in the orphanage I sometimes had a treat of an egg for breakfast."

"Did the orphanage have chickens?"

"I never saw any chickens, and never heard any clucking. I never saw any of the other girls, or even Sister Frances, eat an egg, and I always sat right next to her."

Sister Frances always explained giving Molly May an egg for breakfast because she was three years old and the youngest in the school. The girls stared and made faces at her just the same, whenever she was given an egg. Everyone else had to eat the regular breakfast of gruel and treacle. Molly May wondered where the egg came from when they never saw any chickens.

"Don't worry about the orphanage chickens," Aunt Georgie said. "If you like eggs you will have them here for breakfast very often. Here we are at the stile."

They stepped up and over the stile into the barnyard. What a clatter. The chickens, ducks, turkeys, and geese came fluttering, clucking, squawking, quacking, gobble-gobbling, and honking "Good Morning" to them.

" 'All right, all right, Molly May has come to feed you.' " Aunt Georgie told them.

"Be careful, Molly May, the geese are not always good-humored. If a stranger approaches they set up a racket. See how they lower their head and hiss."

"I think the geese are the funniest of our feathered friends, Aunt Georgie. They wander around, sort of checking everything, while talking to themselves."

"Here we are at the Grain Shed." Aunt Georgie opened a squeaky door and they stepped inside. "In this place we keep the food for all our bird friends." She opened her coat and started filling up her apron's big pockets with grain.

"I'll put in two or three handfuls, Molly May. We'll go outside, then you can dip your hand into my pocket and scatter the grain on the ground. The animals will come running, hopping and waddling to the food."

The chickens and ducks came close to her pecking the food on the ground. Once in awhile one or two would squawk or cackle to

tell a bird-neighbor "move over" or "find your own food". Two or three of them ran away from the food with their morsel so the others would not see what they had found. The turkeys stood quiet and gobble-gobbled. The geese honked and looked at Molly May from a distance. Molly May looked at them too. She didn't like it when they hissed at her.

"Aunt Georgie, do you think Uncle Ed could honk like a goose? They might be so surprised they would stop their honking at us."

"That's an idea, Molly May," Aunt Georgie laughed. "We'll ask him when we go back to the house. While we're here we'll take a quick look for eggs in this building that we call the Hen House."

The door was open so the chickens could go in and out. Molly May followed Aunt Georgie. She saw box-like things against the wall which were the nests where the chickens laid their eggs. But still eggs were found all over the corral in many odd and funny places.

Straw was kept on the floor because chickens like to have dry feet. The straw also helped keep them warm.

"Watch your step Molly May, sometimes you'll find an egg lying in the straw on the floor. You wouldn't want to step on an egg. It could be messy. We don't get many this time of year because it is too cold and it's the hens' resting time."

"I found an egg! I found an egg! Aunt Georgie your foot just missed it," Molly May called out.

"We'll make sure you have that egg for your breakfast tomorrow if you like. I don't see any others now, but the day is

TANGO and PUCK

"Would you like to introduce Molly May to our horses today?" Aunt Georgie asked Uncle Ed.

"That sounds like a good idea. If you're ready for an adventure, Molly May, we'll bundle up and head for the barnyard and corral."

Molly May put on her coat, scarf, warm cap and grabbed her mittens.

"And Ed, don't forget your gloves," Aunt Georgie called. "It's cold. The thermometer reads 35° F."

"I don't know very much about horses," Molly May told Uncle Ed, "but I want to learn. Except for cats and dogs I've only seen animals in picture books." She tried to keep calm, but her insides were shaking with excitement.

A swoosh of cold air greeted them as they opened the door and headed for the corral and barnyard buildings. Molly May's cheeks turned pink as the cold air reached her face. She clapped her mittened hands together to help keep her fingers from getting cold.

"You'll meet Tango, Aunt Georgie's horse. He's white. Puck, my horse, is black," Uncle Ed told Molly May. He took long strides toward the corral. She ran along to keep up with him. "Some of our other horses are in the pasture with our two milk cows. Our cattle, the main animals on the Č Ranch, are out on the range."

"How do you choose a name for the horses?" Molly May inquired.

"Aunt Georgie's horse, Tango, was named because he likes to

prance and dance. My horse, Puck, was named because it is the name of a mischievous elf. Puck likes to surprise me when I ride him. He sometimes stops and pretends to nibble on a tree branch

or bush. Then, all of a sudden, he prances away and soon is in a gallop. He is very smart," Uncle Ed explained.

"Here we are at the corral. We will stay on this side of the stile. I want you to watch the barn ramp ahead of us. I'll call Tango and Puck to come and greet us." Uncle Ed gave two shrill whistles. "Come Tango, come Puck."

Clippity clop, clippity clop, the two horses came out of the barn, down the ramp, and right over to him. "Always talk to animals, Molly May. Horses particularly like to hear a voice. They will lift up their heads when they hear you. You'll notice the sparkle in their eyes if you look closely. Here is a sugar treat for you to give each of them." Uncle Ed reached his hand into his pocket and brought out two sugar lumps. "Put it in the middle of your flat hand and they will lick it up."

"I remember that you let me treat Silver and Claude when you brought me to the Ↄ Ranch from the train in the buggy," Molly May answered as she held out her hand. "That tickled, and they certainly have big teeth just like Silver and Claude."

"We can go into the corral now. Shall we use the stile like we do when we feed our feathered friends, or shall I open the gate?"

"Let's use the stile. I think it's more fun than walking through a gate." The stile had a series of three steps on both sides, which enabled them to pass over the corral fence.

Entering the barn Molly May saw Tango and Puck's stalls where the horses stayed, each in their own, when they were not out in the field or pasture. Molly May noticed a different smell. It came from the oats and other grain in the trough where the horses ate.

"Uncle Ed, I notice a smell here. It's restful. It must come from the horses because they are resting from their work."

"You're right, Molly May. You'll notice several different smells in the barn."

Up toward the ceiling, where the hay was kept, was the loft. Here there was a different smell. It made Molly May remember the beautiful purple alfalfa blossoms which now had become hay.

The next stop was the Tack Room, where the saddles, harness dressing and other equipment made from leather, were kept for the animals.

"I think this is still a different smell, Molly May," Uncle Ed commented.

The other section of the barn was for the milk cows. Uncle Ed milked them every evening and would let Molly May watch the milking some time soon.

"Now I'll show you where our pigs live. Our pigs are not friendly. Never go in their pen, and never put your hands on their fence. You must remember to stay away from the Pig Pen."

"It has been very nice to meet Tango and Puck, Uncle Ed. Will you please teach me to ride a horse? I will remember what you said about the Pig Pen. I'll have enough animals to make friends with, without them."

"I think your learning to ride is a good idea, but we'll wait until the weather is a little nicer. Paint, our horse, is just the right horse for you. She is gentle. You will like her."

Uncle Ed took Molly May's hand as they walked out of the corral back to Aunt Georgie at the ranch house.

SCHOOL

"Aunt Georgie, you're not smiling this morning," Molly May announced at breakfast one cold December day. "Are you sad?"

"No, no." Aunt Georgie replied as she came over and hugged Molly May. "I don't mean to look sad. I'm worried because you need to go to school. I haven't taught school since your cousin Bea was nine years old, back when I taught at the one-room schoolhouse on the prairie." Molly May listened intently.

Aunt Georgie hesitated, "That was where children of all ages attended school from first through eighth grade. I taught them many different subjects like geography, arithmetic, reading, writing, spelling and many more." Aunt Georgie smiled with a far-away look in her eyes.

She hugged Molly May again. "Would you like to go to school if I was your teacher?"

Molly May was surprised. She turned around inside Aunt Georgie's hug and hugged her. She loved school. She'd been learning all about the ⱦ Ranch, almost like school, ever since she'd come to live with Aunt Georgie and Uncle Ed.

When Molly May heard geography mentioned, she became excited. "The older girls in the orphanage loved geography. They told me about the Statue of Liberty, so I knew about it when I saw it in New York Harbor.

"I like to read, and write stories to read to Lizbeth, my doll. I like arithmetic, too. Please let me go to school and you be my teacher."

Aunt Georgie took Molly May's hands and kissed her. "Yes, yes, all right. I'll look over my books and you will start school right here on the Ⱦ Ranch."

A few days later Molly May came running downstairs. "I heard a bell, Aunt Georgie, are we having visitors this early?"

"I thought you would make a better guess, Molly May. That is a school bell. Are you ready to start school at the Ⱦ Ranch?"

"Oh yes! Is geography going to be first? I want to learn about Ceylon where I was born."

Ceylon would be the first geography lesson, but penmanship would come first. Molly May had learned to write at the orphanage, but her notebooks in her baggage showed only pencils were used. With Aunt Georgie she would learn to use a quill pen and ink, first practicing with a pencil. The first marks she would make were circles. It was almost like drawing a picture. If you want to draw a person's head you will have to know how to draw a good circle.

"Since there are a lot of letters in our alphabet, the circle shape is used constantly," Aunt Georgie commented. "With your pencil I want you to do circles like I put on the blackboard."

Aunt Georgie drew many round circles joined close together. "You must use your whole hand and your wrist as you move across the page."

Molly May copied the circles from the blackboard into her notebook.

"That is very good," Aunt Georgie told her. "The next step is push-pull, push-pull. With this exercise you will use your whole arm and hand, not your fingers, keeping your lines the same size and close together. These two writing exercises will help you write

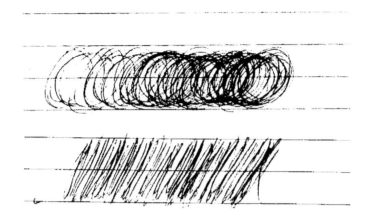

alphabet letters that are a good size and shape for easier reading. I want you to do these two drawings for ten minutes, changing from one to the other as you please."

Ding-a-ling, Ding-a-ling. "I know," Molly May spoke up. "That's a different bell but it means I can stop now."

"That's right. Your work looks very good. On the next penmanship lesson you will use the quill pen and ink.

"I have a very pretty one with a feather on the top which you will use. The pen point that fits on the end of the pen is called a nib. To write, you dip the pen nib into the ink well to get the ink with which to write. You must be careful not to get too much ink or the writing will be full of what is called ink-blots. It takes a lot of practice to be very good with a quill pen, and to keep ink off fingertips, books, and particularly clothes.

"You mentioned that you want to read to Lizbeth, your doll," Aunt Georgie commented. "I know you are able to read books. But it is also important that you learn to write well and be able to read your writing. I think in our writing class you will learn to keep a diary."

A trip to Yellowstone Park was being planned in July. Molly May would write each day what she learned in the Park. She would use her diary to help write a story about the trip when she arrived home.

"I told you I will teach you what I know about the piano," Aunt Georgie said. "Uncle Ed plays the banjo and violin very well. He used to play at the country dances when we were younger. Those instruments are harder to learn than a piano. I want to teach you the piano music for the songs and hymns that you learned at the orphanage because you have a pretty voice. Uncle Ed and I like to hear you sing.

"I will find out what children your age and ability are learning here in America. I want you to like school and to enjoy your lessons."

CHRISTMAS DECORATING PARTY

"Christmas Day will be here in two weeks," Aunt Georgie told Molly May early one Wednesday morning. "It is our turn to have the annual Decorating Party."

Molly May shook her head. "What is a Decorating Party, Aunt Georgie?"

A smile showed dimples in Aunt Georgie's cheeks as she reminisced. For many years the ranch families around Buffalo Gap had joined together to make Christmas decorations on a Saturday two weeks before Christmas Day. They met at a different ranch each year. This year was the ⅋ Ranch turn. Everyone would bring fir and pine tree greens to make wreaths, garlands to wind in and out of stair bannisters or hang around doorways. One of the

favorite decorations was the Kissing Ball made from a wad of paper with chicken wire wrapped around it. Stems of rosemary and mistletoe would be poked into it. When it was hung up anyone who went under it got a kiss by anyone who caught them. Everyone had a lot of fun with the

Kissing Ball.

"I'm going to hide! I don't want to be kissed!" Molly May remarked.

Aunt Georgie turned around, and very quickly gave Molly May a hug and a kiss.

"That wasn't very painful, was it?" she asked.

"Nooooo," Molly May answered shyly, her cheeks turning pink. "I'm just not used to it. No one ever kissed us in the orphanage. But I don't mind you and Uncle Ed kissing me."

"You may get quite a few kisses. Sometimes, in America, we welcome our friends that way. You will get used to it gradually. For now, what color ribbons shall we use?"

"I know red and green for sure, but I love all the colors of the rainbow. Could we use them also?"

Aunt Georgie thought a minute. "I don't know why not. The Christmas Decorating Party has always been very colorful."

The Gilberts were in charge last year and very cleverly made bows from all kinds and colors of ribbons. Everyone used small ornaments to tie on the wreaths or the tree. Families brought their boxes of decorations left over from past Christmas parties. The most important ingredient for the neighbors to bring was love and friendship.

"This party sounds like a lot of fun. I haven't been to very many parties, and never one like you describe, Aunt Georgie. I do remember a party once, at the orphanage. The older girls told me it was called 'A Christmas Party'. A church sent the orphanage a present for each of us, and we were given a little bag of candy. My present was a small, soft, stuffed mouse, but I lost it. I know I'll remember this party!"

"You will need to learn all about Christmas, Molly May. I'll show you how to use big needles to thread and make popcorn and cranberry garlands to hang on the Christmas tree.

"We will need to get the tree and have it partly decorated before anyone arrives. Uncle Ed will go Friday to get it. When he gets it home he will make a wood criss-cross stand for it.

"Ten or twelve ranch families, making sixty grownups and children will come. Philip, Irene and Jean will come the day before to help set up. Some families will bring food. There are always several kinds of cookies. A lot of big and little children will want to play. You already know Sally, Henry, and Arthur Brown. They will come for sure. Everyone gets decoration ideas from each other. It will be a very happy and busy time."

"I just can't imagine it." Molly May turned this way and that looking around the house. "How will everyone fit in here?"

"I heard that, Molly May. You're right," Uncle Ed replied with a chuckle. "I'm off to the machine barn where the party will be held."

The tractor, buggy and wagon needed to be moved out of the barn. Uncle Ed would make tables from saw horses and wood planks. Red and green oilcloth, purchased from the Sears and Roebuck catalog a few months ago, would be spread on the tables to look festive. A few folding chairs had also been bought from the

Sears and Roebuck catalog.

"I'll ask the Hansens and the Johnsons to bring a few of their chairs. Some people like to sit on barrels, so we have a few of those, and the children usually sit on hay bales."

"Oh, it's going to be so jolly, Aunt Georgie. I can hardly wait! Will the grown-ups mind if I peek over their shoulders to watch them making their decorations?"

"My no, Dearie, that is part of the fun; going from one person to another to see what their imagination and creativity has brought out. You may see something you would like to make."

Aunt Georgie bustled around the room looking here and there. "Did you lose something?" Molly May asked.

"No, no! I was trying to choose the next thing to do, to get ready. I've decided to make my special Christmas fruit cake and some cookies. The fruit cake will make the whole house smell delicious. Other families will bring special Christmas foods."

"May I help you with the Christmas cookies? I've helped you in the kitchen with other things."

"That's right, Molly May. I always like your help."

"May I lick the icing pan from the cake? You let me when you made a cake before."

"You really don't 'lick' the pan, but that is what we say. I remember you did a good job with your spoon. Unfortunately, fruit cake doesn't have icing. I'll get things ready now while you tidy your room. When you're finished we'll start our preparations for the Christmas Decorating Party."

A CHRISTMAS TREE HUNT

"It's Christmas Tree time," Aunt Georgie told Uncle Ed at breakfast on Friday. "We'll need our tree early this year."

"There's lots of snow so I'll go on the sled. I'll need a helper. Could you be a good Christmas Tree chooser, Molly May?"

"Oh, yes! Yes! I love riding on the sled, but you will need to help me with the choice. I don't remember anything about a Christmas tree at the orphanage."

Molly May looked quizzical. "Our trees here have no leaves. All the branches look like sticks, but I guess if you put things on them, they wouldn't look too bad."

"A Christmas tree is a very special tree." Aunt Georgie said. "It is called an evergreen because its branches stay green all year long."

To find the tree Uncle Ed and Molly May took the sled to the bluff near Indian Hill. He knew where there was a small grove of beautiful, perfectly shaped, and just-the-right-size evergreen trees. The trees there had nice green branches that smelled good.

They would scramble up the side of the bluff where the trees were. His ax would be needed to cut the tree down. Then his foot would give a push to roll it to the sled. Next Uncle Ed put a rope around the tree trunk and the horses would pull it to the ranch.

"Does this adventure interest you Molly May?"

"Oh yes! I love adventures." Molly May clapped her hands and jumped up and down with excitement. "I know the story of the

Baby Jesus. The Sisters read and taught us a lot about Him. He was born in a stable. There were animals there, too."

"That's true, Molly May. There were also three Wise Men who came with gifts for the Baby. We give gifts at Christmas time to remember Jesus' birthday. We put gifts for the family around the pretty decorated evergreen tree," Aunt Georgie continued. "Get your warm coat, cap, boots, and mittens while Uncle Ed hitches up Silver and Claude to the sled, and away you'll go."

"The bluff with the grove where we usually find our Christmas tree will appear soon," Uncle Ed commented, after they had been sledding for about a half hour.

"Are you ready to scramble up the side of the bluff? It's not very steep. Follow me and step in my snow footprints. I'll try to

take small steps and I'll hold my hand out to you."

They went up a short distance, arriving at a small clearing where many Christmas trees were growing.

"This one is nice," Uncle Ed said as he stroked it. "Look for full branches that go up to a pointed top. Let me know if you spot one. We need one not more than eight feet tall which is this much taller than I am," he said, holding his arms high above his head.

Molly May carefully walked through some trees looking around, fingering and smelling the branches.

"I think I've found it, Uncle Ed", she called. "I'm standing right in it. I hope the lovely smell will go on my clothes."

Uncle Ed came over to her. "You've found a beautiful tree, Molly May. It is the right size. You stand at about it's third, I would say. You will be able to decorate quite a few branches without standing on tippy-toes!

"Now I need to chop it down. You must go over there to be safe."

Uncle Ed took his ax and cut it down. When it was cut and pushed to roll to the sled, they went down the bluff using their footsteps they used to come up. When down, Uncle Ed put a rope around the tree trunk and the horses pulled it back to the house. "Here we are, Aunt Georgie," Molly May called when they arrived home. "Our tree is the greenest, the fattest, the tallest, and the most beautiful in the whole world. Uncle Ed says he'll put the tree's trunk in a bucket of wet sand to help keep it green."

"This tree is very tall, Molly May." Uncle Ed studied it for a moment. He scratched his chin. "I've got it! I'll put a hook in the ceiling and tie the tree top to it. That will help hold it straight."

"Then may we start to decorate it?" Molly May ran and bounced around the room. Her happiness exploded in a cascade of laughter. "Come quick Aunt Georgie. Look at our Christmas Tree!"

"I agree, Molly May, that certainly is one of the loveliest trees we've had. You are an excellent Christmas Tree chooser.

"By the way, if you don't know about Christmas trees then you must not have heard about St. Nicholas or Santa Claus. I'm going to give you a Christmas poem called 'Twas the Night Before Christmas' to read before we start to decorate. It will tell you all about Santa Claus. Most children in England call him St. Nicholas."

Molly May curled up in her favorite pillow-soft chair in the parlor to learn about someone called Santa Claus, and to watch Uncle Ed placing the tree.

WHO IS SANTA CLAUS?

I wonder who is Santa Claus ...

And from what land he comes ...

And where he gets so many toys ...

And such nice sugarplums ...

He comes from ice-bound lands ...

With reindeer swift as light ...

He travels around the world ...

In just one single night ...

He wears a coat and cap of fur ...

At least that's what they say ..

He has merry twinkling eyes ...

And a beard so long and gray ...

And down the chimney softly creeps ...

Without the slightest noise ...

And brings scoldings to all bad boys ...

And the good ones books and toys ...

I wonder who is Santa Claus!

Author Unknown

With just one day before Christmas, Molly May noticed that
Aunt Georgie had quite a few secret talks with Uncle Ed about
Christmas plans. It seemed like Aunt Georgie had been baking,

cooking and decorating forever. The annual Decorating Party had been a success. Jean and Irene and Philip had arrived. The tree did need a few more decorations, but Aunt Georgie said the grownups would finish decorating tonight, Christmas Eve. On Christmas Day, when Jean and Molly May saw the tree they would know Santa Claus had come in the night and filled their stockings because they had been good children. Some presents to each other were already under the tree.

"Did you see Santa Claus, Molly May, where you lived before?" Jean asked.

Molly May shook her head. "I think he only comes to America, and I'm not sure anyone ever sees him. The poem, 'Twas the Night Before Christmas', that Aunt Georgie gave me to read, says he comes on the roof at night when everyone is asleep. I guess we'd better hurry and go to sleep."

"I'm going to stay awake," Jean commented. "Last year I didn't hear a thing, and I stayed awake for a long time. But Santa Claus came because the next morning my stocking was full. I remember I had a big fat orange in the toe. And there were more presents under the tree. It was soooo beautiful!"

Jean looked over at Molly May. "You didn't hear a word I said! You're sound asleep!"

Pretty soon they were both sound asleep. The hours slipped by. The next thing they knew they awoke to a gentle kiss from Aunt Georgie telling them, "Come downstairs to see what has happened in the night." Molly May and Jean flew into their slippers and robes and raced down the stairs. As Molly May skidded around the corner of the kitchen she came to a sudden stop.

There stood the most beautiful Christmas tree Molly May could imagine. It seemed bigger than when Uncle Ed and she had brought it into the house from finding it on their hunt. Molly May didn't remember that it reached clear to the ceiling, covered the big window, and filled the whole end of the parlor. A shining star sparkled from the top of the tree. Little colored birds sat on the tips of many branches. On other branches there were shiny, colored balls.

Very slowly and quietly Molly May walked to the tree. She stared in disbelief. Her lips parted, but words didn't come out. Her fingers gently touched a brightly-colored wooden parrot that sat ready to rock. More toy decorations hid in the branches: a tiny golden horn hung near a small rocking horse, a little stuffed mouse hung by its very long tail that was wrapped around a twig, and there, on another branch was "Ginger Bread Boy". Popcorn, cranberry and silver tinsel strings

were wound in and out of tree limbs.

Molly May turned and ran to Aunt Georgie. They hugged. THIS Christmas Tree was truly the greenest, the fattest, the tallest, and the most beautiful tree in the whole world!

"You better read what this note says that is hanging here before we start," Uncle Ed said as he took a folded paper hanging flat on a branch. He handed it to Aunt Georgie to read aloud.

"HO! HO! HO! MERRY CHRISTMAS! I found you all asleep, and my reindeer are ready to move on as we have many stops to make. Be kind and love each other. Open your gifts, and have a very MERRY, MERRY C H R I S T M A S ! Santa Claus."

"Well, well," Uncle Ed spoke up. "That is a very nice message from Santa Claus. If we all behave I know he will stop by again next year."

"I can smell the turkey cooking," Aunt Georgie commented. "I know it will be delicious, Irene, with your special dressing. The sweet and regular potatoes, vegetables, cranberry salad, and special plum pudding for dessert are all prepared. Dinner will be ready to serve when the turkey and gravy are cooked.

"I think Molly May and Jean have time to open one gift before we eat, so let's gather around the tree and find out what Santa Claus brought them."

Uncle Ed reached under the tree and found a package for Jean from Santa. "What is it? What is it?" Molly May asked as Jean kept squeezing and turning the package around. She finally tore the paper. "Oooh! It's a beautiful doll with long brown curls." She hugged it. "I love her, I love her, she is sooo pretty. Thank you Santa Claus!" Everyone clapped.

"It's your turn next," Jean told Molly May.

Uncle Ed reached under the tree and handed Molly May a large package. She took it hesitatingly, tore a little of the paper and peeked inside. "I can't tell what it is, but it's pretty big. I think I see metal. It is blue."

"Hurry up, Molly May, open it, open it." Jean called out.

"All right," said Molly May as she tore open the package. "Oh! it's a wagon, a wagon just the right size for me," she said. "And look, everybody, the name of it is 'THE OLYMPIC'. It's the same

name of the ship that brought me to America! I love it, I love it," she said as she crouched down and hugged it. "Jean, we can take our dolls for rides in it, maybe you will fit in it, too. Oh! thank you! thank you! Santa Claus. It is the best present I have ever had. I love it, I love it. I will be very, very good next year." Everyone clapped!

"I think the turkey and gravy are finished now. Uncle Ed will carve. Everyone, please take your places at the table," Aunt Georgie said.

"Before we enjoy our Christmas dinner together I want to take a thoughtful moment to share and give our special prayers and thanks for the joy that Molly May has given us by coming into our lives. We have been truly blessed. Amen."

AN ICE ADVENTURE

It was a sunny January 1923 on the $\overset{\text{T}}{\underset{\text{C}}{}}$ Ranch. Six-year-old Molly May had only been in America two months since leaving an English orphanage.

"Put on your warmest woolen stockings, high lace-up shoes, your overshoes with many buckles, and don't forget your mittens, Molly May," Aunt Georgie called. "You are going to ride on the sled with Uncle Ed to get ice from Squaw Creek. It runs along the foot of Indian Hill about a mile from the ranch.

"The summers here are so hot we need an ice box in the house to keep foods fresh."

The ice from Squaw Creek would be kept in the ice house building. It was about the size of a two-buggy building. It had a large pile of sawdust just inside the door. Molly May called it her Sawdust Mountain. She had strick orders not to slide or play on it. On the return from getting the ice Uncle Ed would use the sawdust to pack around the ice blocks to keep them from melting and sticking together.

The ranch also had a storm cellar which was outside the house on the north side. It was a hole in the ground the size of a large closet, about eight feet by eight feet. It had a hinged door which slanted up about three feet from the ground. It opened to twelve steps to the cellar ground. In it were a gunny sack of potatoes, and many squash and pumpkins from the garden. A large stalk of bananas and a gunny sack of yellow cooking onions also were kept in the storm cellar. They were purchased from the Buffalo Gap Country Store whenever Mr. Hanley, the Proprietor, could find them to buy.

"The ice box and storm cellar supplies us with healthy vegetables and fruit the year around," Aunt Georgie commented.

Molly May loved to ride on the sled. She remembered the ride to get the Christmas tree. Her insides started shaking. The snowy ground looked so soft. Even the window panes were frost-covered. Outside everything was covered with snow. Molly May pounded Aunt Georgie with her questions. "Will the sled glide and float over this snow featherbed? Will the rocks and holes in the road under the snow give the sled a bumpity-bump ride? How long will it take to get to Squaw Creek?"

"Silver and Claude, my strongest and favorite team of horses, are already hitched to the sled," Uncle Ed called. "We're ready to go. The snow is deep. The sled will glide along smoothly. Come on, Molly May."

She bounded out of the house. The sled was the same size as the ranch wagon, but without wheels and sides. Uncle Ed had fixed a wooden box for Molly May's seat. He planted his feet firmly on the sled beside her, chirruped to the horses, and away they went.

Silver and Claude flicked their tails and nodded their heads in time with their steps. Their feet made squeaky sounds in the snow. "Uncle Ed, the horses make me think of dumplings because they are plump and bulge in different places."

"I never thought of that description, Molly May," Uncle Ed

laughed as wrinkles crowded around his eyes. "Silver and Claude are very strong. Look, Molly May, look at that big clump of sticks high in that tree ahead of us," Uncle Ed said as he pointed, his breath hanging frozen in the air. "That's an eagle's nest. The eagle is that very large bird floating lazily on the air currents. His dark black wings stand out against the bright blue sky." Molly May's apple-green eyes opened wide.

"I've never seen an eagle. I love birds. I wish I was a bird so I could fly.

"Aunt Georgie said we might see antelope. Have you seen any, Uncle Ed?"

"Yes, as a matter of fact, look to your right, Molly May. Antelope are standing in that clump of trees. An antelope looks something like a deer."

On the South Dakota prairie antelope are often seen foraging for the grass that is under the snow. They have very sensitive nostrils and excellent eyesight.

"When we come closer," Uncle Ed remarked, "they will jump

quickly away. I read they can run up to fifty miles an hour, much faster than Silver and Claude. The only animal that runs faster is a cheetah."

"Oh! I see them. They are a pretty light brown color like the tree-bark. Uncle Ed, you certainly know a lot about antelope."

"We're almost at Squaw Creek. The ice looks perfect for our ice house."

Shadows played games with bare Cottonwood trees and Chokecherry bushes that lined Squaw Creek. The sunlight flickered in and out like a game of hide and seek.

Uncle Ed found a clearing. "Here is a good spot," he said, as he circled the horses and sled around to back it down to the creek's edge.

First Uncle Ed went out on the ice and marked it off into large squares. Then taking a large, wide-toothed saw, he cut out the first block. He gave it a downward push with his foot to shove it into the creek water under the ice.

"Now, Molly May, I have a hole in the ice to get the ice blocks out. Next I will cut all the other marked off places and they'll be ready to put on the sled."

"I can hear the creek talking to me, Uncle Ed. The gurgling sound says it doesn't mind your taking the ice."

"That's good, Molly May, but I think that noisy Magpie bird is scolding me.

"I'm finished. I have sixteen ice blocks on the sled. It will be enough. We can start for home."

Silver and Claude pulled the sled as it creaked, jolted and lurched slowly along with the heavy load. The late afternoon sun made the ice look like sparkling jewels.

When they arrived back at the ice house, Silver and Claude slowly inched the heavy sled back to the entrance door. Uncle Ed lifted the ice blocks off the sled with his steel ice tongs. He placed the ice neatly on a carpet of sawdust and piled one on top of another with sawdust between.

"My Sawdust Mountain is disappearing, Uncle Ed," Molly May told him, as he threw a tarpaulin over the ice and closed the door.

"The ice blocks will keep well, Molly May. With luck this ice will be enough for Aunt Georgie's ice box all summer."

"Thank you, Uncle Ed." Molly May hugged him. "It was fun.

NEW COUSIN

"Good morning," Aunt Georgie greeted Molly May. "I'm glad you're up early because today is going to be very special. Your new cousin is six weeks old. He is to be baptized today. This means he will be given his name, Edward Anders Griffin, the same as Uncle Ed's name."

Philip, Irene, Jean, and her baby brother will come this morning. Everyone will go to Buffalo Gap to a church for the baptism. The parents will give him to God in prayers, and he will become one of God's children."

"Why are they giving him away?" Molly May bombarded Aunt Georgie with questions. "I thought they just got him! Doesn't he belong to them anymore? I'll take him if no one wants him. Is the baby the one for Jean to play with? She told me her Mummy was getting a baby for her. We wanted you to get one for me so we would have two babies to play with. I forgot to ask you before. Aunt Georgie, will you please get me a baby?"

"I'm sorry, Molly May, I can't do that, but you will see baby Edward often. You and Jean can play together with him. I can't explain 'God' to you right now. When you go to Sunday School you will learn about God. Today we need to get dressed and be ready to go to Buffalo Gap for the baptism. I want you to wear one of the dresses cousin Bea made."

Mid-morning, Philip and his family, in their horse and buggy, arrived in the front yard. Aunt Georgie greeted them, and peeked excitedly and cautiously at the baby. Molly May was right at Aunt Georgie's heels, peeking at the new baby.

"He is so tiny, Aunt Georgie, and not as pretty as Lizbeth, my doll. Jean and I don't want to play with him."

"That's not a nice thing to say at all, Molly May. I'm shocked."

"I can't help it, Aunt Georgie, that's what I think." Molly May's eyes clouded up. "I'm sorry."

"Never mind right now. You and Jean may play in your room for an hour or so until it is time to leave."

"Bring your doll, Jean, and we'll play house with Lizbeth," Molly May suggested.

"I have her." They walked upstairs. "You look very pretty in your blue party dress," Jean said, as she took off her coat. "I didn't wear a party dress."

"Why don't you put on my pink one? I remember that you liked it. Then we'll be like sisters. Be sure to put on the panties and petticoat to match. Our dolls can have a rest-time while you change."

"Are you sure it's all right, Molly May?" asked Jean as she put on the dress.

"Yes, I think my dress looks lovely on you, Jean, but it is a little long. It doesn't show the matching petticoat, and the panties

80

are supposed to show when you jump or swing around. Aunt Georgie keeps her sewing box in the next room. She keeps her scissors there. I can cut some material off the bottom of the dress.

"I found the scissors! Stand very still while I take a look." Molly May scowled as she held up the hem. Her hand went to her chin as she thought a minute. "Aunt Georgie made one of my dresses shorter, but she didn't cut it. I better do what she did. She said she would sew it, and then I could wear the dress next year, also.

"Stand still some more, Jean. I'll get a needle and thread. I can do like she did if you stand very still."

Jean stood as still as a cat watching for a mouse.

"Turn around a little bit, then stand still again," Molly May told Jean. "There, I think it's done. Let me see, turn all around very slowly while I watch. Yes, it looks all right even though the very full skirt made some lumpy places. Look in my mirror on the closet door. Do you like it?"

Jean walked over to the mirror. "Oh, it 's so pretty. Let's pretend we are taking our dolls to a party," Jean exclaimed. "We both look like we're going to a party."

"I think you look very pretty, Jean. You may have my dress for keeps. Would you like it? Aunt Georgie has bought me so many dresses. They are all beautiful, but I don't know when or where I'll wear them all."

"Oh yes, I love it. If you're sure you don't want it."

"Now that my dress is your dress, we will be sisters instead of just cousins. I found out that everything has a sister. The Olympic ship I was on, to come to America, had a sister. Because both ships looked like each other they were called 'sisterships'. The other ship's name was The Titanic. When you're wearing my other dress, we will look like each other. That will make us sisters."

* * *

"Come girls," Aunt Georgie called. "Put on your coats. It's time to go to the baptism."

Molly May and Jean put on their coats and walked down stairs.

"What good children," Aunt Georgie exclaimed. "You're already in your coats and ready to leave. Molly May, if you like, you may ride in the buggy with Jean, the new baby, and Irene and Philip. Uncle Ed and I will see you at the church."

When they arrived they joined several family friends who came to attend the baptism. Afterwards many of them went back to the ⅃ Ranch for a celebration party.

A HULLABALOO

"Hang up your coats, children. Molly May, please set the table," Aunt Georgie said as she turned to Jean. "Your Mommy wants ..." she suddenly let out a scream. "JEAN, what dress have you got on? The skirt is all bumpy." Jean started to cry, tears cascading down her face. Aunt Georgie took her hand, and said quietly, trying to calm Jean and herself. "What has happened to Molly May's 'Cousin Bea's dress'? Let me look."

When she took a good look she saw that the hem was sewn up to make the dress shorter! It was even short enough to let the matching petticoat be seen. As Jean jumped around she also noticed the dress had been made short enough for even the panties to show. "Did Molly May do this?" she asked.

Molly May, hearing all the noise, came into the parlor to investigate. "I gave Jean my dress, Aunt Georgie, so we could be sisters." Molly May looked at Jean. "You look so pretty. Aunt Georgie will let you have it. I fixed it to fit you like Aunt Georgie made one of my dresses fit me. It was easy."

"I don't know what to do with you, Molly May. Cousin Bea will faint when she hears about this escapade."

Molly May's eyes brimmed with unshed tears. "The look-alike dresses make us look like sisters. I love Cousin Bea's dress and I love Jean, too. She looks so pretty because the dress is so pretty. I only need one party dress. Please let her have it, please." Her voice lowered to a whisper. "I didn't mean to be naughty. I don't want a spanking."

"What is going on with all this discussion." Irene asked as she came in from the bedroom where she had been nursing baby Edward. "Oh, heavens to Betsie, Jean, whatever are you doing wearing that beautiful dress Cousin Bea made. You must get back in your own clothes right away. The bottom of the skirt looks rather odd." Irene hesitated a moment, then she said, "As a matter of fact, you do look very pretty in it."

Jean, crying, ran over to Molly May. "Take it off me, Molly May. Help me take it off. Mommy will spank me."

The parlor door opened letting in a wintry breeze. "Well, ladies and children, Philip and I heard a commotion. What is all this hullabaloo about?" Uncle Ed remarked. "Aunt Georgie and Irene are looking very upset. But I see a little four-year-old girl who is looking very, very pretty all dressed up for Baby Edward's baptism party. And Molly May must be her sister since they look alike. Come over here girls so Philip and I can hug both of you."

Jean and Molly May could hardly get over to them fast enough so each could be smothered with hugs from strong arms.

"Ladies," Uncle Ed continued. "If I'm guessing right, I think things will work out just fine. Right now things should be kept just the way they look. Aunt Georgie and Irene are both good seamstresses. I expect Molly May and Jean will stay look-alikes in the beautiful dresses they are wearing. When the delicious and nutritious dinner is cooked, we'll be ready for baby Edward's baptism party. Meanwhile, I'm going to pronounce this Hullabaloo is over!"

Guests were arriving for the baptism celebration. Many brought food to add to the dinner. The house looked very festive as some of the Christmas decorations were still up.

Aunt Georgie announced that dinner would be ready in one or two hours. The children could play outside, play dominos, or their favorite card game of Go Fish at a card table in the parlor while the grown-ups enjoyed visiting.

"Mother", Sally Brown asked, "Molly May, Jean and I want to go on the swing and the teeter-totter, if that's all right with you. Please call us for dinner because the swing is at the back of the house."

"All right, be careful and don't swing too high."

"Yes, mother, I'll be careful. Mother always worries about me," Sally told Molly May. "Does your Aunt Georgie worry about you?"

"I think she does. I haven't had much time or chance to go on the teeter-totter because I only have Jean to play with when she visits, but I use the swing a lot. Aunt Georgie keeps me busy with my school work that I like very much. Do you like school?"

"Yes, I'm in third grade and I love to read. I learned to read in second grade. What grade are you in?"

"I'm in all the grades, I guess. Aunt Georgie told me she was a teacher for all the grades through eighth grade when her daughter, Bea, was in school. But that was a long time ago. I love school and I think Aunt Georgie is the best teacher in the whole world. I went to school in the orphanage, but it was never like Aunt Georgie teaches me."

"I'm sorry to break up your teeter-totter fun, girls," Mrs. Brown came and told them, "but our dinner is almost ready. I know how you like to set the table."

"Don't worry, Molly May, mother likes to tease me about setting the table. Here we come. Molly May and Jean, I'll race you to the house."

PORCUPINES

"If you ever see a porcupine on his back, Molly May, I want you to let me know," Uncle Ed remarked one day.

"That is a funny way to want to look at a porcupine, Uncle Ed. Of course, you wouldn't get his quills in your face like Popeye does. Why do you want to see one like that? Do they lie on their backs?"

"I guess they do sometimes," Uncle Ed answered. "I read recently that they are as helpless as turtles on their backs. I'm soft-hearted when it comes to animals. I don't like to see them in trouble. If on their backs makes them helpless as turtles, that puts them in a bad spot."

Molly May remembered the first time she saw Popeye's face bristled with porcupine quills. It made her cry. She knew it must have hurt. The quills stood out on his face like a big bristly broom.

But later it was worse. Uncle Ed had to tie Popeye down on a board and do his best to remove the quills with a pair of pliers.

Molly May ran into the house. She didn't want to see Popeye, and Uncle Ed also, hurting. She knew that the quills were very sharp and stiff. Sometimes they were covered with the porcupine's hair.

"Why does Popeye go near a porcupine?" Molly May asked.

"He is a very smart dog. Doesn't he know that he can get hurt by that little animal?"

"We don't understand it either, Molly May. When Jean's Daddy, Philip, was little, here on the ranch, we had a couple of dogs. Porcupines are often found in brush, and a dog seems to know when one is there. It didn't matter which of our two dogs was with us, he would attack. He would try to bite the porcupine and the porcupine just humped his back and immediately fired an astonishing assault of quills at the dog. The dog would immediately wind up with his face covered with porcupine quills. You could tell he was in agony."

It was a heart-breaking job for Uncle Ed. He had to remove the quills the same for Popeye as he did for Philip's dog. Because the quills were quite poisonous, they needed to be removed very quickly since they could be fatal within a short time. The quills were the porcupine's defense against his enemies. Dogs became their enemies when they chased them in the brush, so the porcupines were prepared to shoot their quills at them.

"Just be sure you leave a porcupine alone if you see one, but call me if he is on his back!"

GROUNDHOGS and EGGS

"Happy Groundhog Day, Molly May", Uncle Ed remarked one wintry morning.

"That is the funniest 'Happy Day' I have ever heard," Molly May answered. "How are we going to make it happy? And what is a groundhog?"

"Groundhogs are small animals sometimes called woodchucks. They live in the ground. They look similar to our prairie dogs that you have seen. The groundhog is quiet, he doesn't make a bark-like noise like our prairie dogs."

February 2nd is always called Groundhog Day. The groundhog is considered to be a weather forecaster. If the day turns sunny, the groundhog will see his shadow and there will be six more weeks of wintry weather.

"It would be better for us to take our eggs to market during colder weather. So we hope the groundhog sees it's shadow.

"I've been busy making out a grocery list," Aunt Georgie called. "The money we receive from selling the eggs will help pay the grocery bill. Molly May, I'll need more eggs to fill the crate."

"I'll find more, Aunt Georgie. I know where the chickens hide them. They cackle to tell me where: bok, bok, b-cok." Molly May made a chicken noise. "Then I find the eggs in the woodpile, in the manger, hay loft, in high weeds next to the barnyard fence, in their nests of course, and even some in the pig sty. But I know not to go there because our pigs could be dangerous."

"By the way, Molly May," Uncle Ed remarked. " Do you know that two pigs in one pen will often eat more than two pigs in two pens. They stuff themselves just to keep the other one from getting the food."

Molly May started giggling. "That is a very funny story, Uncle Ed."

"It is true, Molly May, no matter how funny. When you find more eggs, you may help Aunt Georgie sort, count and crate them. It takes time to count all the eggs because our crate holds twenty four dozen. While you are doing all that, I will hitch up Silver and Claude. You may go with me in the wagon if you like. We'll take the eggs to Mr. Hanley who owns the Buffalo Gap Country store."

"What is he going to do with that many eggs? How can he tell if they are all good -- some might be rotten."

"They will have to be candled," Uncle Ed told her.

Candling is holding two eggs in each hand and alternating them from each hand, Mr. Hanley would hold the egg up to the light. This would show him if the egg was fertile or too old. Next, he would quickly transfer the second egg in each hand up to the light. If good, the four candled eggs would be placed in individual partitions, into a new crate. Mr. Hanley would repeat this process until the whole crate was candled. "I don't recommend you try candling, Molly May," Uncle Ed commented.

To get to Buffalo Gap it was a jiggly-joggly wagon ride over a prairie sea. The same land was covered with coarse grasses for miles and miles. It was mostly level with an occasional rolling rise. If there was a tree it meant there was water from a small creek, often completely dry in summer. Silver and Claude pulled the wagon past the Bale Family fenced ranch lands. Uncle Ed and Molly May could see the Bale house in the distance. Groundhog Day weather stayed cloudy as Uncle Ed had wished, although the charcoal colored sky threatened rain.

Molly May had been to the Country store once before, but she was still interested in investigating some more. She remembered there were many bolts of pretty yardage material. Aunt Georgie said she would let Molly May pick out a bolt and she would make her a new dress. But Molly May had to not talk back to Aunt Georgie to deserve the new dress. If she didn't behave she would get a spanking.

Last time Molly May had been at the Country store there was a bright colored wooden bird on a swinging perch in a cage. She hoped it was still there. It was in the window next to the store door. When the door to the store opened it would jar the cage and make the perch swing.

One whole side of the store, toward the back, was filled with metal tools of every description. Uncle Ed went to look at them .

"Remember, Molly May," she heard Uncle Ed call. "I promised you that you could pick out only one chocolate Mound from Mr. Hanley's wooden candy barrel. We want you to have good teeth."

She went over to the large barrel filled to the brim with chocolate covered vanilla flavored thick cream candy called Mounds. After gazing at them for awhile she could not decide, so she sang out: 'Eenie, meenie, miney, mo. To which chocolate Mound should I go'. She picked up the one her finger touched, and took a tiny bite.

"Thank you, Uncle Ed," she called. "My finger picked out a delicious one. It's sooooo good!"

Aunt Georgie had given Uncle Ed her grocery list, so as soon as Mr. Hanley finished candling the eggs he handed over the list to be filled. "Bill, I figure you know what shelf holds what, so, if you don't mind, I would appreciate you filling Georgie's list."

"All right, Ed, but I need a helper. I understand your young niece, Molly May, knows how to read and write. Molly May, can you write on my pad the name and price I tell you? If so, I would like you to be my helper. We'll go from shelf to shelf. I'll tell you the name of the item and its price, then I will place it in a big bag."

"Oh, yes, Mr. Hanley! I learned reading, writing, and arithmetic in the orphanage. I'll write carefully so you will be able to read everything, but you might need to help me with spelling. I will love being your helper."

"I need to interrupt a minute," Uncle Ed said. "Molly May will do an excellent job, I'm sure. I'll get out of your way, Bill. If you want me I'll be checking out your tool section while you and your helper work. By the way, Georgie's list is long, I may need to use the money I get from the eggs to pay for part of the supplies.

"Very good, Ed. The eggs will be fine. We've bartered before.

"Let's start, Molly May. There will be some things that need weighing and wrapping. I'll put them in a separate bag. We'll take them over to the big wooden counter when we're through. That's where I keep my scale, cash register, brown paper bags, roll of wrapping paper, and ball of string."

Aunt Georgie had a very long list, but Molly May and Mr. Hanley were soon checking everything at the wooden counter. There were five big boxes of groceries filled to the top by the time they finished.

"Here is the sugar treat ready for Silver and Claude before we start for home," Uncle Ed reminded Molly May.

They were now ready to start the jiggly-joggly, prairie sea wagon ride back to the Ⴆ Ranch.

"The groundhog did see his shadow," Molly May announced, "so it was a very happy Groundhog Day. Thank you Uncle Ed. "

PAINT

The month of March had started. Aunt Georgie had promised Molly May that she would celebrate her three-day birthday like she did in England - March 13th, 14th, and 15th.

"For your seventh birthday celebration, Molly May, you don't have to recite Sister Frances' five statements," Aunt Georgie told her. "I will be the judge, and you have passed. We want to give you a choice of something special for the first two days, March 13th and 14th. The third day, March 15th, we will give you our present to start off your 'Happy New Year'."

"That sounds like a much nicer three days than I had at the orphanage. May I make my choices now?"

"Yes! Be very careful because a special choice once made is the same as a wish once made - it cannot be changed."

For the 13th of March Molly May chose that Aunt Georgie would make her favorite dinner, roast beef and Yorkshire pudding because everybody, except orphanage children, ate this dish very often in England. Aunty Belle had cooked it for dinner the day before she took her to the Olympic ship to sail for America.

For the 14th of March Molly May chose that Uncle Ed would take her on his horse, Puck, for a bareback ride to bring in the cows for milking. He had done this once before and Molly May thought it was a lot of fun. The milk cows' pasture was not far from the house. On the side near the house there were bluffs. At their base a small creek gurgled. It kept the grass moist on the sides, as well as furnishing a welcome sip for the cows. The ground was gently sloping on the other side .

Aunt Georgie and Uncle Ed both spoke: "Your March 13th and 14th choices have been granted. Today is March 15th. To see our Happy Birthday gift, and to start your 'Happy New Year', come outside and see our present to you. It is waiting patiently."

Molly May raced to open the door. She looked around. "Only Paint is standing here, Aunt Georgie and Uncle Ed." Molly May looked around a little bit more. Then, very slowly, in a quiet, hesitating voice, she asked, "Is Paint my Happy Birthday and Happy New Year present? Is Paint really going to be MY horse?"

"Yes, Molly May, Paint is now your very own horse. You have ridden her a lot and we think she should be yours."

"I can't believe Paint is really mine." She hugged and stroked her. When Paint put her head down Molly May leaned her head on hers and clung to her. "She's soooo beautiful."

Paint's face was colored with a white blaze from her ears to her nose which set off her eyes, one blue the other one brown. Her mane was a solid dark brown. Her coat was chestnut interrupted by one large patch of white on her hind quarters, and a white sock on her left hind leg.

"May I get on right now? I don't need a saddle, I can ride bareback."

"Well, it looks like Paint has replaced us in Molly May's affection," Uncle Ed laughingly remarked to Aunt Georgie.

"No! No!" Molly May told them, "but I had to hug and stroke

Paint to let her know I love her and she is really mine. Thank you! Thank you, Aunt Georgie and Uncle Ed. I do love Paint, but I love you more." She hugged and kissed them. "May I bring in the cows for milking this evening?"

"I expect you may in a day or so, but first I want you to go with me a few times," Uncle Ed said. "I want to teach you how to get back up on Paint should you slip off accidentally, particularly when you ride bareback because a horse's back is slippery.

"When your cousin, Philip, was a boy he slipped off more than he stayed on, so I was glad I had taught him how to get back on by himself, when he was alone."

After Aunt Georgie's special birthday dinner there was a birthday cake with SEVEN candles on it. Molly May made a wish and then blew them out. Then Molly May and Uncle Ed went out riding.

"Are you ready for your lesson?" Uncle Ed asked.

"Oh yes, Uncle Ed! It will be special, but better than the first time I rode Paint. That was a little scary."

"All right, young lady," Uncle Ed started, after dismounting.

"First, after you slip or fall off, you must wait patiently until the horse puts her head down to nibble at the grass. Then you gently put your left leg over Paint's neck holding her mane tightly, nudging her gently with your foot. When she raises her head high you will be able to slide down her neck and be aboard again. Always be sure you use your left leg otherwise you will be facing the wrong way, and turning around would be tricky. Don't forget, a horse's bare back is slippery.

"If you fell off, Molly May, do you think you could get back on that way?"

"I don't know, Uncle Ed. I think your instructions will make me be very careful NOT to fall off. I don't want to practice it either."

"Another day I want to tell you some good points how to take care of and treat Paint. You will be completely in charge of her! We'll finish our ride for now. The cows are all ready on their way to the barn. They know when it's milking time. Aunt Georgie and I can separate after I finish milking."

"No! No! Uncle Ed!," Molly May hugged him. "I don't want you to separate. I want you both to stay here with me."

Uncle Ed started to laugh. "Molly May, you are a funny little girl. I was referring to the machine we use to separate the cream from the milk."

Molly May began to giggle. "I forgot all about that machine. Aunt Georgie has even let me turn the handle sometimes." She let out a long sigh. "I would cry if you and Aunt Georgie left me or sent me back to the orphanage. I"ll always try to be very, very good."

NIBBY

Prairie dogs were in abundance on the Ⱦ Ranch. They wouldn't hurt a person and they didn't do too much destruction to the vegetable garden. The Ⱦ Ranch welcomed the little burrowing animals that always seemed very happy gnawing and biting whatever they could find.

"Did you know we have two prairie dog towns on the Ⱦ Ranch?" Molly May asked one morning. "I'm going to name the prairie dog town that is near the house, 'Friendly Town'. The animals seem to be very tame since they are used to us walking past them every day. They don't quickly run away down their holes when anyone passes. Have you noticed how they stand up, look us over, and bark a greeting, Aunt Georgie? May I have a prairie dog for a pet?"

"I don't know why not. I remember when Jean's Daddy was a little boy your age he had a pet prairie dog. He called it 'Wheee'. You should have a baby one so you can raise it to be tame. I'm not sure how you will get it. We'll ask Uncle Ed."

The other prairie dog town Molly May called 'Unfriendly Town'. It was the area in the field next to the corral. When you came close to them the prairie dogs quickly scurried away into their burrows. Molly May quietly watched them. In a short time one or two peeked out of their hole showing only a part of their heads. Soon a little more of their body showed, and they became brave and barked.

99

"Uncle Ed, would you get me a baby prairie dog for a pet? Aunt Georgie says I can have one if I can get it. She said cousin Philip had one when he was my age. She said I need a little one so I can raise it and it will be tame."

"Yes, I remember Philip and his pet. We took a big pot of water and poured it in their hole. It didn't hurt them, just made

them come out to see what was happening. First, the old ones came out and then the youngsters. I think I can catch a little one for you. Philip had a special recipe to feed his. Aunt Georgie probably put it somewhere in her

cookbooks. You can help her hunt for it."

Molly May went looking for Aunt Georgie. "Oh! There you are. Uncle Ed says he will try to get me a little prairie dog for a pet, but we must find the recipe for its food. He thinks it is in one of your cookbooks. May I hunt through them?"

"Yes, I think we called it 'Wheee's food'." I expect it will be under miscellaneous."

"I found it! I found it! I think this is it. I'll read it to you: 'Mix together one tablespoon honey, a smidgen of salt, and a cup of warm milk.' I think that sounds pretty good, Aunt Georgie. I also have a name for my pet. I'm going to call him 'Nibby' because on the prairie they look like they are nibbling when they eat. Do you like that name?"

"I think that name is very appropriate. Let Uncle Ed know you found the recipe, and we will make up some right away to be ready for the new addition to our household when Uncle Ed catches one."

Molly May tried to be very patient. For one whole day she never mentioned prairie dogs.

"Uncle Ed, I saw several prairie dogs today," Molly May casually remarked the next morning.

"That's nice," Uncle Ed answered, but didn't say another word.

Molly May stood a few minutes watching and waiting for him to say something more. But nothing! So she skipped away to check both prairie dog towns. Several days went by with no conversation about prairie dogs. Molly May was sure Uncle Ed would try to catch one for her. It was very hard not to talk about prairie dogs.

It was a whole week later when Uncle Ed called to her. "Molly May, today is prarie dog day," he said. "I have baby Nibby prarie dog right here for you. He is very young. We will keep him in this cage I made for him for a few days. It will help teach him this is his new home. You may gently take him in and out and pet him so you become friends."

"I'm sooooo excited, Uncle Ed. Thank you! Thank you!" She carefully picked up Nibby, held him calmly and stroked him.

With all Molly May's tender loving care Nibby became tame and grew very quicky. It didn't take long before the little prairie dog became everybody's special Ⱦ Ranch pet.

SPRING PICNIC

It was late April. Uncle Ed's alfalfa field that was close to the house was so pretty that Molly May wanted to run and play in it, but it was the playground for bees. Aunt Georgie said she might get stung. The purplish alfalfa flowers were everywhere. They smothered the field, making a mass of solid color.

"Today we'll go to the annual ranchers' Spring Picnic," Aunt Georgie told Molly May.

"The same ranch families who attended the annual Christmas Decorating party will be there. Philip, Irene, Jean, and baby Edward will come from their Southfork Ranch. Your friends from the local ranches will all be there to play with. Twenty to thirty families come every year.

"Philip and his family have arrived," Aunt Georgie said. "They will go in their wagon. Uncle Ed has hitched Silver and Claude to the buggy, Molly May. You and I will ride with him. Do drive carefully, Ed. I don't want my banana cream pie jiggled. It's for the food auction."

"What's an auction, Aunt Georgie?" Molly May asked.

"An auction is considered sort of a game. At the picnic auction the men offer a price for the food item they want. Perhaps another man also wants that item. So he will offer a bigger price. When there is only one person left bidding, he pays the highest price he bid and gets the item.

"Uncle Ed always tries to buy my banana cream pie because it is his favorite," Aunt Georgie remarked. "The auction is a lot of fun."

The picnic grounds at Buffalo Gap were sixteen miles from the Ȼ Ranch. Thick clumps of cottonwood trees that grew along the banks of a small creek gave plenty of shade at the picnic. The children could wade in the creek. The large open grassy area was perfect for the anticipated games.

"Here we are," Uncle Ed said as he reined in Silver and Claude. "Everyone out, let's go."

All the ladies got busy with the picnic lunch. "Molly May and Sally," Mrs. Brown called, "Please put these knives, forks and spoons at place settings. Jean, you may put napkins at the places.

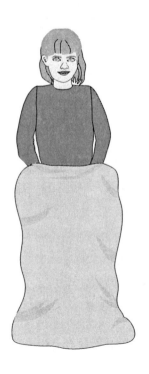

Henry and Arthur can put the plates on the tables because they are heavier to carry. We will unwrap the various salads and fancy looking dishes."

After the auction and lunch the ladies got busy cleaning up the tables. "It's fun time now!" someone shouted.

"We want the Sack Race! We want the Sack Race!" many children called.

"We're going to start the Sack Race for the children,"

one of the men in charge announced. "Come, all you children. Come to the picnic tables area to get your sack."

"Molly May and Jean, come on," Henry and Arthur yelled.

"I'm joining the race. Come on, Jean." Molly May took her hand as they ran to the picnic tables to get their sacks.

"Go to the starting line," the announcer explained to the children, "and get into your sacks. Hold the sack up around your waist. The idea is to hop to the finish line without dropping the sack or falling down. If the sack drops, or you fall down, pull the sack up and continue in the race. The first one to reach the finish line will be the winner.

"ARE WE READY? HERE WE GO! One for the money, two for the show, three to get ready and four to GO!" the announcer shouted.

"Come on Molly May. You can do it!" Uncle Ed yelled. "Come on, Jean, hop, hop," yelled Philip and Irene.

Both Molly May and Jean fell down and got up, helped each other between giggles, fell down and got up, and continued with their giggles.

"That was fun, Aunt Georgie," Molly May said, after the race had a winner.

"I don't think I could ever win that race," answered Jean.

"Now that the children have had some fun let's look at the automobiles three of the ranchers brought," Philip suggested.

"Yes, let's," Aunt Georgie commented. "Ed wants to look at them. He would like to check them out. We will need one for our planned trip to Yellowstone National Park in July."

The cars were parked near the two outhouses, but at a safe distance from the horses with the wagons and buggies.

"In case you and Jean go to look at an automobile, Molly May, keep your distance," Aunt Georgie warned. "You never know what this new contraption will do on its own."

"May Jean and I play with Henry and Arthur Brown while you look at the cars, Aunt Georgie? That would be more fun for us."

"That's a good idea, we'll find you at the play area when we're through."

Aunt Georgie and Uncle Ed remembered last year's picnic when there was quite a bit of excitement surrounding the automobiles. One of the men announced that Mrs. Burnett was going to drive their new car home.

A commotion started. Unfortunately, Mrs. Burnett started the car a little faster than she intended. She took off in a blast of deafening engine noise as she backed into the edge of one of the outhouses instead of going forward. The car's back bumper hooked the edge of the outhouse step. She tried, frantically, to stop the car, but in her excitement she drove forward pulling the outhouse behind her.

There was a male occupant in the outhouse. He started yelling and cursing Mrs. Burnett. She and her automobile continued dragging the outhouse about fifty feet before she was able to stop.

Besides the occupant's racket, everyone was trying to tell Mrs. Burnett what to do. Finally, with plenty of help, the men got the automobile and outhouse separated. Poor Mrs. Burnett was very embarrassed so the family left as soon as possible, with Mr. Burnett driving. It was very fortunate that no one was injured.

"The Burnett occurrence caused quite a hubbub," Uncle Ed remarked. "These cars have a good sized back bumper. You certainly have to be careful what you bump into! I can't tell too much seeing them here. I'll have to make a trip, one of these days, to Rapid City to look them over. I hope you'll join me, Philip."

"Absolutely, Dad, I wouldn't miss a trip like that!"

"That's a good idea, Ed," Aunt Georgie agreed. "Now I think we better check on the children at the play area."

"Aunt Georgie, here I am up in a tree not very far from you," Molly May called when she saw her. "Henry is up here, too. Arthur took Jean to the creek to wade."

"You better climb down now. Be extra careful! We'll get Jean and Arthur at the creek. We'll be leaving soon."

The afternoon passed quickly. Everyone enjoyed sharing the picnic foods, visiting with each other, and joining in various activities. "There are always chores to be done on a ranch," Mr. Brown commented. "I think it is time for us to head for home. Be careful, Henry, when you skiddle down your tree."

"Picnics are a lot different in America, Aunt Georgie. The orphanage took the children on a picnic once, but we never had things happen like last year's picnic or this picnic today. I think the Spring Picnic is the best one in the whole world," remarked Molly May.

HAYING

One of the never ending chores on a cattle ranch is putting up hay. The Ⴛ ranch workday began at sunup and continued until sundown. Uncle Ed had five hired hands on the Ⴛ ranch. It was considered a large Cattle Ranch. A rancher never tells his accurate acreage. It would be like telling someone how much money you have in your bank account.

Seasons dictated the time for the varied work on the Ⴛ Ranch. In addition to his grazing acreage, Uncle Ed had several hay fields for cattle fodder. His machinery was not the latest in design, but when it came to doing the job, it got the job done.

Spring on the ranch began any date in April or May, depending on the whims of the weather. Spring time meant many new lives would arrive; feathered friend babies running about, piglets in the pigpen, and calves in the pasture. Seeds of corn, oats and barley were planted. Turkeys roamed the alfalfa fields with just their heads and necks showing above the grasses as they hunted for grasshoppers. At night they would roost in the Cottonwood trees.

"The alfalfa is in full bloom," Uncle Ed remarked one day in late June 1923. "We will be cutting soon." This meant summer was here. Somehow he always knew when the alfalfa would be ripe, which meant it would be perfect cutting and haystacking time.

Out from the barn would come the mowing machine. Silver and Claude were strong enough to do a good job of pulling the mower and, a little later, the raker. Bunching meant putting the hay into hay cocks to get the hay ready for loading in the hayrack.

After the raking and bunching was finished two of the men who were hired helpers pitched the hay from the hay cocks into the hayrack. Another man, standing in the hayrack, kept the hay pressed down.

When the hayrack was a full load it was hauled by Silver and Claude to the haystack building area. The hay, again, had to be pitch-forked from the hayrack and pitched into a nice shaped haystack. Molly May knew she would now be allowed to watch the haystacks being made. Haying was hard and tiring work, and most often done during hot summer days.

"I hope you had a recess, Uncle Ed," Molly May asked. "Aunt Georgie gives me one from school. She says I do better work if I rest once in awhile."

"No, Molly May, when we put up hay we don't get a recess, but I'll tell you about one day when we certainly did.

"There is a thermometer on the back porch of the house. Everyone kept an eye on it, but didn't fuss when it was 100° F or even 102° F. But this particular day it registered 106° F. "I think it is too hot to work, turn the horses out and go home," I told the men. That day, Molly May, I guess we had a recess!"

Haying on the ₺ Ranch lasted many days. "Molly May," Uncle Ed said one morning. "Today you may come and watch the men make a haystack. You will have to sit down in some hay, not too close to the workers or the equipment."

This day haying activities were close to the house. One of the hired hands had a black dog with the not so clever name of "Blackie". Dogs had not been in Molly May's life until she came to live at the ranch. However, she had become used to playing rough with Popeye. Unfortunately, she started rough housing with Blackie. The next thing she knew, she was hearing a noisy growl and a jaw-snap noise that caught skin close to her right eye enough to tear the skin. Molly May started to yell and scream, holding the right side of her face. She was frightened!

Uncle Ed jumped down from the hayrack, noticed a little blood on her upper cheek, picked her up, and hurriedly carried her to the house.

As soon as Aunt Geogie heard what had happened she found Merthiolate in her medicine chest and quickly dabbed Molly May's eye. "Ouch, Aunt Georgie," Molly May cried and screamed between dabbs. "That stings, that hurts!"

"I must wash your eye, Molly May. The Merthiolate will disinfect your eye injury and the area around it to keep you from getting an infection. I want you to lie still, and the Merthiolate will make it better. I know your eye will feel better very soon."

Uncle Ed came in to see how Molly May was feeling. "Molly May, I think you may have pulled Blackie's ear, or done something he did not like. He is not used to having children around. I am afraid he is not a very friendly dog. Aunt Georgie was very quick to put something on the area to keep infection down. We will watch your eye very closely. We are sure it will feel a lot better very soon.

"You were a lucky little girl. Dog bites can be dangerous. You may come again, in a day or so, to see how the haystack is being made, but stay away from Blackie," he consoled and warned her.

YELLOWSTONE, WEEK ONE

"Aunt Georgie, I'm scared," Molly May whispered. "Will we go over the cliff into the river?"

"Just sit quietly, Molly May. We'll be all right," she answered reassuredly. Suddenly she screamed.

"Eeeeeeee! You're right on the edge, Ed!"

"Now Georgie," Uncle Ed replied in his usual calm voice. "Stop fretting. The road has a foot on either side of the car. When we meet another car there's a place here and there where we can back up or pull up to pass."

These words offered little comfort to Aunt Georgie. When she wasn't screaming she closed her eyes, gritted her teeth, squeezed her hands together and prayed.

It was July 1923. Uncle Ed, Aunt Georgie, and Molly May were driving on the Cody Road, a narrow, twisting, cliff-hugging dirt ribbon. It followed the beautiful Shoshone River through Shoshone Canyon in Wyoming. They would make camp at Mammoth Hot Springs, the northern entrance to Yellowstone National Park. The trip, 500 miles from the $\bar{C}$ Ranch in South Dakota, would take five days.

In preparation for the trip Aunt Georgie and Uncle Ed had read many books about the park to Molly May.

"I loved the stories you and Uncle Ed read to me," Molly May commented.

"I heard that, Molly May," Uncle Ed said. "Tell me what you

found out!"

"The books said the wilderness was beautiful. It explained about the geysers, and it told how the 'Grand Canyon' of Yellowstone was formed. The books also warned about bears, not getting too close to them and not feedng them, keeping campsites clean, and keeping all food in safety boxes."

"That's a very good recollection, Molly May. You were a good student. I predict the trip will be wonderful," answered Uncle Ed.

Uncle Ed had made a box the full length of the running board step of the 1923 Studebaker Touring Sedan. In it went the kerosene

lantern, an ax to chop wood for the campfires, fishing poles and tackle, car tools, extra oil for the car, a gas can in case the car ran out of gas, and Aunt Georgie's newest, most prized possession, her Sears & Roebuck canvas bag packed full of aluminum dishes.

The car was bulging with boxes and bundles. Aunt Georgie kept thinking of one more thing she knew they would need. Uncle

Ed kept thinking of one more thing he knew they should leave behind.

Molly May looked on in amazement. "I'm going to take my doll, Lizbeth, and most importantly, my diary to write down what I like and think about the park," she said.

On the car radiator hung a canvas bag filled with water to take care of the motor in case it over-heated.

The bedding was wrapped and rolled in a large tent, securely tied on top of the trunk at the back of the car.

Aunt Georgie had purchased what all campers should wear, as stated by the Sears & Roebuck catalog. She wore her new mid-calf khaki skirt with matching jacket, a beige blouse, a visor cap, and no-nonsense sturdy walking shoes. Uncle Ed wore breeches for the trip. They tucked into his just below the knee laceup boots. His brown sweater and wide brimmed cowboy hat, which was creased on four sides, completed the outfit. Molly May had khaki bloomers that came just below her knee, a matching long-sleeved blouse, khaki knee socks, and brown laceup shoes. She sat in the back seat sandwiched between the boxes of food supplies. To see the passing scenery she looked through the isinglass car windows.

At Mammoth Hot Springs, the beautiful large terraces looked like giant steps. "I can hardly believe my eyes, Aunt Georgie. Their pools all have different shades of yellow, orange, green and brown. I remember one book said the colors were formed from tiny living bacteria and algae living in the very hot water."

One late afternoon when they returned from the Mammoth

Hot Springs terraces Uncle Ed commented, "It looks like our neighbor campers have had a visitor, and I expect it was a bear."

The campers were very disturbed at the mess they saw on their return. They had left everything on the table including boxes of miscellaneous food. It looked like the bears had thoroughly enjoyed themselves. All the boxes were broken into and the contents were scattered everywhere. Some things were even thrown

up into the low tree branches. The campers evidently had not read about keeping their camp clean or about the animal life in the park.

The disturbed campers gathered up what they could salvage and left.

"I hope those untidy campers are not going to our next campground," Molly May remarked. "If they do, do you think the bears that had so much fun will follow them, Uncle Ed?"

"Well, you never can tell. We'll see!"

YELLOWSTONE, WEEK TWO

Their next camp site, at huge Yellowstone Lake, was about fifty feet away from another camper.

Yellowstone Lake was known for its shallow, sloping, sandy bottom. This made wading easier for fishing.

"Georgie, we have enough kindling and wood for our campfire. I'm going to go fishing for our dinner. Everyone says the Cutthroat Trout are plentiful and delicious, besides being a challenge for fishermen to catch," Uncle Ed said.

He rolled up his breeches and waded quite far out. Before long he came back to the camp with a nice catch of fish for dinner.

"Molly May, it's time to set the table for our supper," Aunt Georgie told her.

"Are you sure this is a safe place to have our table?" Molly May questioned. "There may be a geyser or hot springs in the ground from all the smoke billowing and blowing."

"It's safe, Molly May. The campground areas are well checked by the Rangers. I'm glad you are learning about this interesting park."

When they all finished cleaning and safely putting their food away so the park animals could not get at it, it was dark enough to stargaze.

"I see the Big Dipper already," Molly May called. "Do you see it, Uncle Ed? It is very bright. Aunt Georgie taught me a little about the stars. She said the Big Dipper has seven stars."

"I'm looking for the Great Bear, it should be near the Big Dipper," Uncle Ed answered.

The stars were bright at the Ⱦ Ranch, but here they shone even brighter. Here Molly May felt if she grew a little taller she would be able to touch them.

That night was particularly clear and beautiful as the moon was full. "Do you recognize that howl you hear, Molly May"? Uncle Ed asked.

Molly May listened. She turned her head one way, then the other. "Yes, it's a coyote just like we hear at the Ⱦ Ranch."

"That's right. Let them sing you to sleep."

"May I sleep outside tonight, Aunt Georgie? You can keep the tent flap open. I will call you if I wake up."

"No, Molly May. I don't want you to sleep outside the tent. You are very sweet. There might be some night bugs that would find you tasty so they might nibble you. You're a very sound sleeper, so you might not feel them."

"That's funny, Aunt Georgie. I know you're teasing me."

"Yes, I'm teasing you. Save your sleep-out night for the Ⱦ Ranch. Good night, sweet dreams. We'll be going to bed shortly."

During the night Aunt Georgie suddenly woke up screaming, "A bear, Ed, a bear! He's out there! Get him!"

"Calm down. Georgie! You'll wake Molly May! Go back to sleep! I expect some bears are around, but our camp site is clean. It won't interest them." Before he finished speaking Georgie had turned over and was asleep again.

Uncle Ed, Aunt Georgie and Molly May saw many bears and other animals, but they always kept their distance. "Of all the animals I've seen, Uncle Ed, the buffalos are my favorite," Molly May told him. "They give me the giggles when they lie down in dust patches rolling and kicking up their legs for their dust baths. Then they stand up shaking out the dirt and dust from their fur coats. That really makes me laugh!

"And remember when our car was very close to a moose? We looked at him; he looked at us. Then he opened his mouth and I saw his very large teeth. I think his teeth were bigger teeth than those of Silver and Claude on the ranch. He gave me more giggles."

"I'm glad you are enjoying the animals, Molly May, but now we

will visit the section of the park that has more interesting and larger geysers, particularly Old Faithful which is the most famous geyser," answered Uncle Ed.

YELLOWSTONE, WEEK THREE

The next day they spent their time visiting shooting geysers and more fizzing hot springs in what was called the Grand Group.

"These geysers scare me with their bubble-bubble, hissing, and sizzling sounds," Molly May said. "They shoot hot water and steam high into the air. Some make noises like a gurgle way down deep in your throat, some just cough, and some only give a little hiccup. Some smell like rotten eggs. My favorites are the geysers that give off little puffs of fleecy steam that curl gently up from colored pools," she told Aunt Georgie.

Fearless Geyser gave off a sudden swoosh of water. The edges of the beautiful pools were covered with minerals from the overflowing , sloshing hot water.

"Aunt Georgie, I think the geysers play a guessing game. I wonder if they will erupt, now or later, spout very high or just a little?" questioned Molly May.

The Firehole River was not far from Old Faithful. On its bank was a geyser called Riverside. When it erupts it shot water out over the river.

Molly May learned that Grand Geyser shot higher than Old Faithful but only every two days. It was a quiet, usually clear pool, but then very suddenly blasted out water two hundred feet up into the sky.

Old Faithful had been named because it always erupted twenty five to twenty eight minutes apart. People said it had erupted thousands of times, the year round, since its discovery in 1870.

"I hear it! I hear it! Uncle Ed I hear it! I hear a low gurgle and some water hiccuping out of Old Faithful's mound," Molly May shrieked gleefully.

Suddenly there was a loud swish and water, steam and spray flew into the air. "It must be one hundred fifty feet high in the air,"

Uncle Ed remarked. There were four or five great spurts of water, graceful sprinkles of spray and steam, and then it abruptly stopped. The water that had been high in the air moments before, was now running in every direction, off Yellowstone's grey-white mound. Uncle Ed tapped Molly May's shoulder, "Molly May, close your mouth and stop looking skyward. Old Faithful's show is over for at least a half-hour, then it will perform again. We will come back to see it."

"I like geysers better than the hot springs." Molly May commented. "The rainbow-colored algae around their edges is so beautiful. Uncle Ed, these geysers and hot springs names are my favorite: Witches Caldron, Black Growler, Fearless, and Thud Geyser."

At Emerald Group they saw Handkerchief Pool. "Young lady," a Ranger said to Molly May, "put your handkerchief into the water." It was sucked away, then in a few minutes it reappeared again all nice and clean. "I'll help you rescue your handkerchief," the Ranger said. He put her hand in his to help her hold a short rod attached to a chain. The rod picked it up, and Molly May's handkerchief was retrieved

The next adventure was Biscuit Basin that had 'stone cookies', two to three inches wide, floating in the pools. They were made from minerals hardening from the evaporating water.

In all areas there were signs telling people to be very careful to stay on the boardwalks. Some areas around the geysers were not strong enough to hold a person's weight. One spring was called "Skeleton Pool" where many animal skeletons could be seen through the clear water. The animals had fallen off the boardwalk into the spring.

Mammoth Paint Pots were hot springs that had become choked with fine clay. They looked like bowls of boiling pink, grey and yellow mud made by the sulfur and iron in the mud.

"Next we will visit Roaring Mountain," Uncle Ed announced. "My notes state that this side of the mountain has steam popping and hissing out of it." While they looked at it, three deer came along. The deer gingerly picked their way across the side of the mountain. They knew not to step where steam would come out and burn their dainty hooves.

Their last campsite was Yellowstone's Grand Canyon which contained the Upper and Lower Falls. The park received its name when discoverers saw so much yellow stone on its banks. "The Canyon drops one thousand to fifteen hundred feet to the river below," Uncle Ed said. "The canyon cliffs look like different colored cans of paint were dropped on them," Molly May commented. Aunt Georgie said, "It took the river many thousands of years to chip, nibble, carve and gobble away the rock walls to make this canyon."

The day before their visit ended they went to Yellowstone's Grand Canyon with a ranger. He took them quite close to the edge and pointed to an osprey nest perched high on the tip-top of an old dead tree. When the mother flew away they looked through field glasses to see three babies shuffling places in the nest.

The next day it was time to drive home. After five long days Uncle Ed, Aunt Georgie, and Molly May finally rounded the bend in the road and saw the Ȼ Ranch. The hired hands, left in charge, said all the animals missed them and everything was in good shape. Popeye came bounding to them with a warm, wet, licking welcome!

After seeing many animals in their natural setting, and the beauty of Yellowstone National Park, Molly May knew the trip would stay in her memory a long time. It was truly a land of discovery and wonder -- a trip to always remember!

A CHANGE

It was late August. The sun streaked through the windows onto Molly May's bed. "I'm awake, I'm awake," she sang out. "It's going to be a beautiful day. I'm sure something exciting is going to happen today."

"Dress and come down to breakfast," Aunt Georgie called. "Uncle Ed has finished his early morning chores. We are waiting to have breakfast with you. We are going to have a family discussion."

Molly May scrambled into her clothes and flew down the stairs until she came to the last three steps. "Oh! Oh!," she spoke her thoughts outloud, a frown giving her face a questioning look. "I must walk quietly downstairs, not like a charging bull, I still could be sent back to the orphanage." Her pace changed to a lady-like walk.

"Good morning, Aunt Georgie and Uncle Ed," she said quietly, giving them each a kiss. "I think it's going to be a beautiful day,"

"Yes," they both replied. "We're sure it will be a beautiful day, and a very busy one as well. We have been talking about your future schooling. We are both getting older, and it is time for Uncle Ed to retire," Aunt Georgie said. "We are planning to give Philip, our twenty-five-year old son, the ₡ Ranch. Our land connects with Southfork, his present ranch. He is young and can manage more acres for his cattle along with ours. We are planning to move to Hot Springs where you will go to school."

The house in Hot Springs was only thirty miles away. It was

owned by Aunt Georgie. Her parents had both died the year before Molly May arrived. They wouldn't have to take much from the Ↄ Ranch except immediate supplies like clothing, bedding, and of course food supplies. The Hot Springs house was just as the parents left it since no one had lived in it.

Molly May sighed with relief. They were not going to send her back to the orphanage.

All Molly May's special books and school things from her room would be packed along with all her furniture.

"I don't want to give up the Ↄ Ranch school," Molly May said tearfully. "I will be very sad to leave here."

"Don't be sad, dear." Aunt Georgie hugged her. "I expect we can make a study room some where in the Hot Springs house. We will also come back to the Ↄ Ranch for visits with Philip and his family."

"You won't be giving up school, or your furniture. We'll see to that." Uncle Ed said. "You will have a new teacher and be with a lot of other children like yourself, all learning new things. I know you will like school very much because you are interested in everything."

"You will still have homework to do," Aunt Georgie chimed in. "We will be in the new house together, so you will have us both to help you with any questions. And we do have a surprise for you. We will take the piano with us. We've made arrangements for you to take lessons from a very nice lady who knows more about playing the piano than we both do. Would you like that?"

"Oh, yes, Aunt Georgie. I don't want to stop learning the piano."

"Your new school will be very different from our ⟨ Ranch school. There will be many other children with you, both boys and girls. You will be in a class with children your age. You will study several subjects like you have done with me, but new ones also.

"You'll find the Hot Springs house quite different from the ⟨Ranch," Aunt Georgie continued. "Instead of sleeping downstairs, like Uncle Ed and I do here, the two bedrooms and sleeping porch

Hot Springs Elementary School in 1923, now a museum

are upstairs."

"Oh! A sleeping porch. Let it be for me, please, please." Molly May started jumping up and down with excitement. "I can guess what it is like, and I love the outdoors."

127

"Very well, you may have the sleeping porch," Aunt Georgie told her.

"Then everything is agreed. All we have to do is start packing some boxes. I'll help you with yours first, Molly May, then you may help me with mine. I know Uncle Ed can handle his with no problem. Philip and his family will start moving in after we leave.

"Our next adventure will be 'Molly May in School at Hot Springs'!"

REMEMBERING

"Wake up, Molly May," Aunt Georgie called. "We're going to Hot Springs in our 'Yellowstone chariot'." Ever since the trip to Yellowstone Park Aunt Georgie had called the car by that name. "We need to check the Hot Springs house to find out what needs to be done and what to take with us before we make the move in a few days."

As Molly May dressed, the sunrise from her open window spilled strawberry-jam-colored-clouds across the yard, while the wind rattled softly through the cottonwood trees.

"Are you ready?" Aunt Georgie called again. "We'll eat a quick breakfast and be on our way. By the way, I've been wondering if you would like to make a list of a few of your favorite or unusual memories of your life on the Ⱦ Ranch that you hope will continue during your new adventure in Hot Springs?"

"Oh Aunt Georgie, I'll love making a list. I have many thoughts of my days here."

"That's good, but not too long a list, perhaps four or five happenings."

"I'll start thinking on our ride to Hot Springs. I want it to be a surprise to you and Uncle Ed."

"Are we all set?" Uncle Ed called. "If so, Georgie, you and Molly May climb in. I'll crank our 'Yellowstone chariot' and we'll be on our way. It will take over an hour to go the thirty miles to Hot Springs. I don't want to speed too fast."

Molly May knew one happening she would never forget, but she didn't want to have that scare ever again. Molly May had ridden Paint to get the cows from the pasture to the barn for milking. It was a lovely sunny day, and the bells on the cow necks shook a pretty sound as they chewed the grass. Suddenly Paint stopped short. "What's the matter, Paint?" Molly May asked. She bent to pet Paint's neck and saw her first rattlesnake on the ground.

"Come on Paint," she said while giving a nudge of her foot on Paint's side and a pull on the reins, "Let's get away from here. We'll get Uncle Ed, he will need to get the cows in today because that rattler scared me. He was all coiled up and rattling fast and loud. He sure wanted us out of his way." It was a good thing Uncle Ed had warned me that I might see a rattlesnake in the pasture some time.

Not wanting to think of the scary rattlesnake anymore, Molly May turned her thoughts to happier memories. As she wrote them down on her list, she smiled.

1. Will the sunset make pictures with magic colors behind the clouds like it does at the **C̶** Ranch?

2. Will I hear many different birds chirping and chattering?

3. Will there be a birdbath and birdfeeder to fill

like I did on the ⅂ Ranch?

4.   Will I find dandelion puffs to blow and scatter to the wind? You take a big breath, pout your lips, blow, and swoosh, the dandelion puff is gone.

5.   Will the Hot Springs chicken dinner smell and taste as good as the ⅂ Ranch chicken dinner?

"I'm finished with my list, Aunt Georgie. I'll read it to you when we get to Hot Springs."

"Very well," Aunt Georgie replied. "I see the house, we're almost there."

***